# Making Wines
## Liqueurs & Cordials

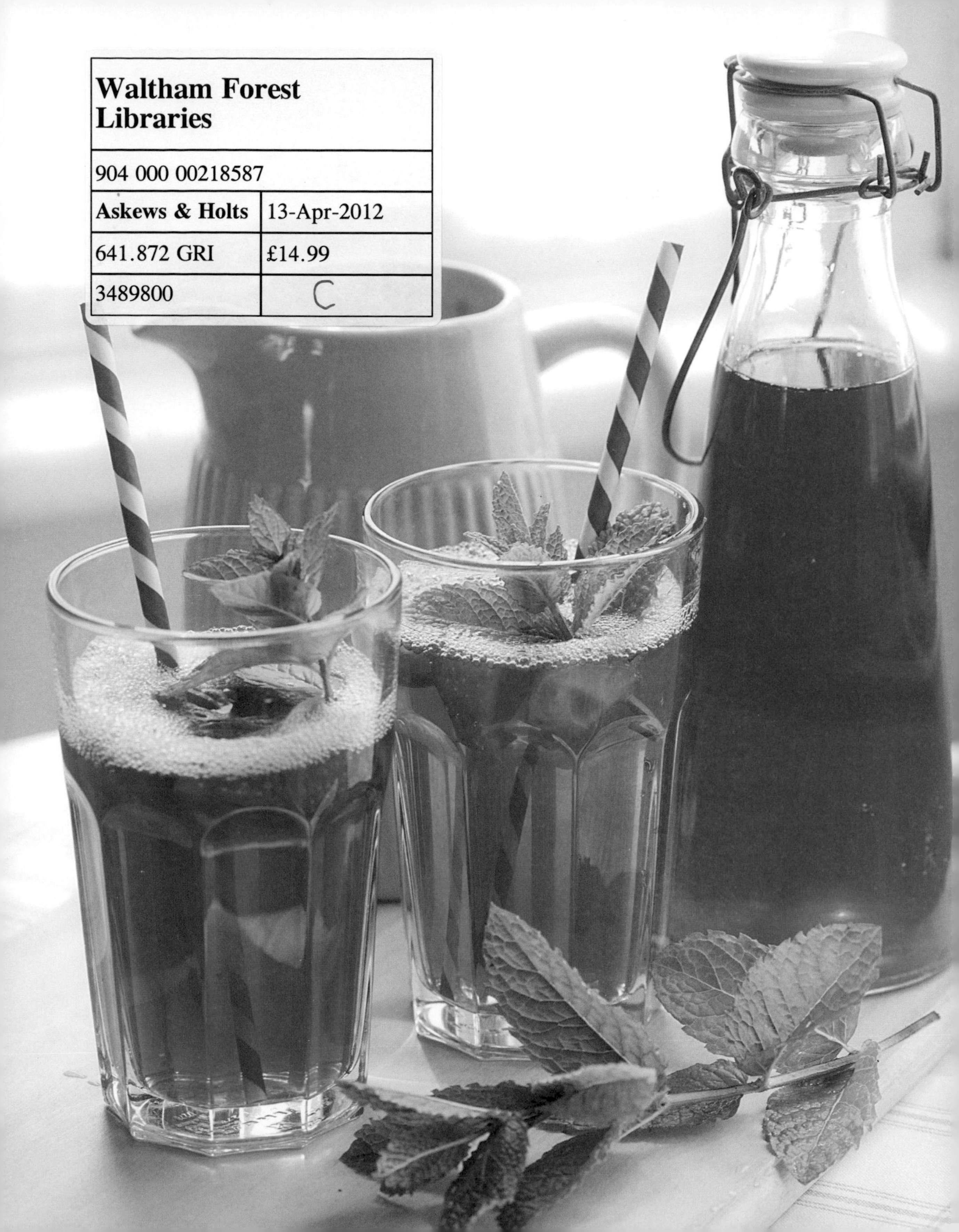

# Making Wines
## Liqueurs & Cordials

101 delicious recipes using natural ingredients

### BESHLIE GRIMES

**CICO BOOKS**
LONDON NEW YORK

Published in 2012 by CICO Books
An imprint of Ryland Peters & Small Ltd
20–21 Jockey's Fields      519 Broadway, 5th Floor
London WC1R 4BW       New York, NY 10012

www.cicobooks.com

10 9 8 7 6 5 4 3 2 1

A CIP catalog record for this book is available from
the Library of Congress and the British Library.

ISBN: 978 1 908170 23 1

Printed in China

Editor: Eleanor Van Zandt
Designer: Roger Hammond at bluegum
Photographer: Gavin Kingcome
Stylist: Sophie Martell

## Measurements

Both American standard and metric measurements
have been used in this book. It is most important
not to mix the two systems, as two measurements
are not always exact equivalents. Note in particular
that there is a significant difference between the
"gallon" yield in the Wine recipes, which is a
U.S. gallon (3.785 liters) and the 4.5 liters yield
provided for British readers (equivalent to a
U.K. gallon); this difference is governed by the
size of demijohn available in these countries.

Note:
1 teaspoon equals 5ml
1 tablespoon equals 15ml
A cup equals 236ml
A quart (U.S.) equals 0.946 liter

# Contents

# Introduction

As a child I clearly remember the effort that my parents and extended family put into tending their fruit and vegetable gardens. They maximized every inch of space, and nothing went to waste. We would often spend an evening shelling peas: putting the peas into one pot and the pods in another, ready to be transformed into pea-pod wine.

We also enjoyed gathering free produce from the countryside. We would spend many a warm late summer/ early autumn day picking wild fruits from the hedgerows and foraging for all sorts of things, from mushrooms to hazelnuts— even nettles. To us children it was akin to finding treasure. These were my first forays into using up gluts of fruit and vegetables and experimenting with other free goodies.

Quite a few memories from friends and family contributed to the writing of this book—recipes, too. I delved back into my grandparents' handwritten recipes, some of which I have shared with you here. There were some good stories about the trials and tribulations of wine making. My all-time favorite was from an uncle who was himself a keen wine maker. He had come to the end of his wine-making year and had carefully organized the results of his labors. The bottles were labeled and stored on their sides along the tops of his kitchen cabinets. While lying in bed one night, he and his wife heard a loud bang from the kitchen. Then another and another. On arriving in the kitchen they were confronted with what only can be described as a wine fountain; and the floor was awash with wine! Somehow there had been a chain reaction, which had caused all of the wine to explode from the bottles. Not surprisingly, my uncle did not participate in the yearly wine competition held with the rest of the family.

I would like to thank my family and friends not only for all of their weird and wonderful recipes and ideas (some used here, others not) but also, most of all, for their critical eye and endurance in sampling the syrups (or cordials, as they are called here in England), wines, and liqueurs.

A lot of hard work goes into growing your own fruit and vegetables—or even picking or selecting the desired ingredients. The last thing one would want is to have any wastage. Sometimes using up a glut can be a little testing. You can freeze or store fruits and vegetables and make them into jellies, jams, and chutneys, as I do, but you may still find that you've got some left over. When I first started making wine, it was simply to use up this excess—really just an afterthought. Now I still freeze fruit and vegetables or store it fresh, and I still make jams and chutneys, but I will always make sure I have plenty of produce for making syrups (cordials), wines, and liqueurs. Every year I will make a batch of wine or liqueur to be ready for the following year.

So I recommend that you always have a pot of wine yeast and nutrient (see page 16) stored in your kitchen, ready for times when an unexpected glut of fruit will come your way, so that you can make the most of this good fortune. Then, even in the depths of winter, you can savor the taste of summer as you enjoy its fruits long after they have been picked.

As you progress in making your own country drinks, be brave and experiment with different flavors and combinations; you may produce an original drink with its own unique taste. Even if you stick to the recipes, though, you will probably find, as I do, that no two batches of a drink will ever turn out exactly the same. Don't think of this as a failure; it is, rather, part of the charm of this traditional country craft.

# Techniques

## Sources of fruits

You can find fruit and herbs for your drinks in many places, from your own garden to your local supermarket.

### Garden

Nothing is quite so satisfying as planting, nurturing, and harvesting your own sun-ripened fruit and preserving its flavor in wines and syrups (cordials). The list of fruit and herbs that the amateur gardener can grow is almost endless (although, of course, success with a particular plant will vary depending on the region or hardiness zone in which you live). I love to pick fruits when they come into season and then use them in almost all types of food and drink, from ice cream to my favorites, country wines.

If your garden's fruit-growing possibilities are limited (or you haven't got a garden at all), see if a neighbor, friend, or relative can offer you some; many people find themselves with a glut of a particular fruit and are happy to share it. You may be able to offer them, in return, some produce from your own garden—so that everyone enjoys greater variety—or simply a bottle or two of the delicious end product.

### Countryside

Plenty of fruit is to be had free from the countryside in late summer and early fall. Where I live, in England, the hedgerows are fairly groaning with it at this time of year. Keep your eyes open for elderberries, blackberries, and raspberries. (Remember, though, that elderflowers appear in late spring.) If you are lucky, you may even find crab apples and rose hips. A warning: avoid picking fruit alongside a busy road, where exhaust fumes will damage it, or at a low level where dogs might target it.

### Farmers' markets

Ideally you'll have access to a thriving farmers' market. These are a fabulous source of locally grown ingredients. You may be able to find some wonderful honey (perhaps for making my Honey and Lemon Syrup [page 66]) or bunches of lovage or even potted scented geraniums. If you have difficulty finding a particular fruit or herb that you need, always ask; even if none of the producers have what you are looking for, they will probably know someone who does.

## "Pick Your Own"

I absolutely love going to a PYO farm. It's a great day out, especially for the kids; we pack a picnic lunch and make a day of it. Apart from the fun, though, the main attraction, of course, is the relative cheapness and quantity of the fruit—and the quality. Maybe not all the fruit will be uniform and beautiful, but they will most definitely have the fullest flavor. This is the next best thing to growing your own. Most PYO farms will have the usual strawberries and raspberries; try to find one that offers other varieties, such as loganberries or tayberries.

## Supermarkets

Many people depend on supermarkets for citrus fruits and other hot-climate produce. There is no harm in this, but when it comes to some of the other fruits, I do find that a lot of it is rather tasteless compared to the locally grown options discussed above. On the other hand, most supermarket fruit is fairly inexpensive, so if you want to make large batches it makes sense to add some supermarket-bought produce to your own freshly picked fruit in order to obtain the quantity that you need.

# Selecting and preparing ingredients

The effort you put into sourcing and selecting fruit, herbs, and flowers should match the effort put into actually making your chosen drink; this will give you the best results. Careful handling of these ingredients will also yield dividends.

## Choosing fruits, herbs, and flowers

When buying fruit, you'll naturally select healthy specimens, and if you've picked your own, you'll need to give it the same critical eye before actually using it. Look out for any fruits that are rotten or look less than appetizing, and discard them. You need to use your judgment to ascertain whether the fruit or herb that you have picked is good enough to go into your chosen recipe. When using elderflowers, avoid brown ones; instead, look for lovely creamy white, open flowers; pick shiny, plump rose hips, as opposed to the ones that are starting to dry out. As a general rule, pick more fruits and herbs than you'll need for the recipe, to make sure of having enough usable ones. In recipes containing lemon or orange zest, I have specified unwaxed fruits, as it stands to reason that if you are zesting them you will not want to add wax as well. When picking flowers such as the elderflower or rose petals, I suggest waiting to harvest these at the end of a warm day to allow their perfume to be at its strongest.

## Washing produce

Any fresh ingredients you buy or pick will need washing before use. When washing soft fruit, such as berries, take extra care not to squash the fruit, as you would lose the precious juice needed for your chosen recipe. Berries can be placed in a bowl of water and then gently scooped up with a sieve, allowing the water to drain out. I give fruit that has a rind, such as oranges and lemons, a scrub with warm water, as these may have been sitting on a supermarket shelf for some time. Herbs can be rinsed under cold running water to remove any insects. The most difficult ingredient in this respect is elderflowers. Once picked, the stems can be gently shaken to remove any large insects; however, you will find that the elderflower will retain quite a few smaller ones. Place the elderflower in a bowl and leave it outside for an hour or so to allow most of the remaining insects to crawl away. You will not be able to eliminate all of the insects at this stage, but when you strain the liquid through fabric (see page 12), any remaining insects will be removed.

# General techniques

## Sterilizing

The job of sterilizing your equipment is the most important one when making wines, syrups, lemonades, and liqueurs, and I cannot place enough importance on this part of the process. Fortunately, there are some fantastic products on the market that are ideal for this job.

**Sterilizing a demijohn** If a demijohn is especially dirty, start by placing a capful of bleach straight into the jug and then fill it to the very top with hot water. Leave it overnight, tip away the water and bleach solution, and then rinse the demijohn thoroughly; wear old clothes as it may splash a little. Next, use special sterilizing powder, following the manufacturer's instructions: pour the powder into the demijohn and fill it to the top with water. Leave the solution in the jug for the required time (normally 15 minutes). Finally, empty the demijohn and rinse with fresh water. It will now be ready to use. If the demijohn is not very dirty, you can omit the overnight bleaching stage.

**Sterilizing a fermenting bucket** Proceed as for sterilizing a demijohn. Other equipment to be sterilized, such as bottles and jars, can be submerged in the bucket with the solution and left for the required time (again, 15 minutes is usually sufficient). Rinse with fresh water.

**Sterilizing bottles for other drinks** The sterilizing powder used in wine making can also be used for bottles you are using for syrups, lemonades, and liqueurs. Just mix the solution with water in a large bucket, using the proportions specified by the manufacturer.
Use a pitcher (jug) and funnel to fill each bottle completely to the top. Pour away the solution after the required time and rinse as usual.

Alternatively, if using preserving jars, you can sterilize these in the oven, shortly before you need them. Wash them in hot, soapy water, then rinse in clean hot water and leave on a dish towel to air-dry. Lay the jars on their sides on the top shelf of the oven. Heat the oven to 225°F (110°C, gas mark ¼) for 20–30 minutes.

## Straining

Most of the drinks in this book must be strained at some point to remove material, such as pulp, from the liquid. For this you will need a sieve or fabric and a suitable container to collect the liquid.

> ### Measurements
> Both American standard and metric measurements have been used in this book. It is vital not to mix the two systems, as two measurements are not always exact equivalents. Note in particular that there is a noticable difference between the "gallon" yield in the Wine recipes, which is a U.S. gallon (3.785 liters) and the 4.5 liters yield provided for British readers (equivalent to a U.K. gallon); this difference is governed by the size of demijohn available in these countries.
>
> Note:
> 1 teaspoon equals 5ml
> 1 tablespoon equals 15ml
> A cup equals 236ml
> a quart (U.S.) equals 0.946 liter

**Muslin** A large square of fine, soft muslin (or other loosely woven fabric, such as cheesecloth) is great for straining, as it can be folded for a fine strain or just left as a single thickness piece for a quick strain. Buy a generous amount of fabric; it should be relatively cheap, so that you can discard it after use without a qualm. You can use this by itself, tied up around the edges and suspended over a bowl, or use it to line a sieve.

**Jelly bag** This is just a shaped bag, with three or four loops to hang it by, and sometimes comes with a framework of legs, for suspending it over a bowl while the juice drains out, leaving you free to carry on doing something else. The fabric is a little thicker than the

Straining raspberry syrup using a sieve and a funnel.

aforementioned muslin and so can give a finer strain. Also, the bag can be washed many times. The only disadvantage is that these bags can be rather expensive.

**Sieve** A sieve, or strainer, is essential, as it can be used either by itself, for an initial strain, or lined with muslin to produce a clearer end product.

## Storing

Various kinds of storage space are suitable for different drinks and production stages.

**Cool, dark place** This can be any place that is away from the fluctuations of your heating system and, of course, relatively cool. An old-fashioned pantry, or larder, is ideal; or you might use a corner of your basement or garage. The space under a stairway (if in a cool part of the house) is another possibility. The darkness also ensures that you are able to maintain a good color in your finished syrups, liqueurs, and, especially, wines.

**Refrigerator** The fridge is a good place to store your syrups and lemonades once they are opened, but you do not need to place any of your homemade wines or liqueurs in the fridge unless, of course, you are chilling a white wine.

**Storing wines** Once your wine stabilizes (that is, once fermentation has stopped) and it has cleared, it can then be bottled up. However, if you prefer, you can leave it in the demijohn/fermentation jug: just replace the air lock with a rubber bung and store the jug in a cool, dark place. If you do decide to bottle up the entire contents of the jug, siphon the wine into sterilized bottles. The bottles must be filled up to a third of the neck of the bottle, so that about 3/4 inch (2cm) of air space will be left below the cork. Make sure to use new corks, and insert them fully, so that they are level with the top of the bottle. Special plastic corks with a lip will facilitate this. Store the bottles on their sides in a cool, dark place.

## Freezing

Both syrups and lemonades can be frozen. I like to freeze them in ice cube trays and, once they are frozen, place the cubes in a freezer bag and label. I find that I have less wastage than when using larger containers, and the cubes are the perfect size for an individual serving.

Diluted syrups and lemonades make wonderful ice pops (ice lollies). Freeze the liquid in molds or little plastic party cups, placing the sticks in the middle when semifrozen and then freezing them until solid.

# Wine making processes

The following processes apply to one or more of the types of drink you will make by using the recipes in this book.

## Fermentation and temperature

Fermentation is a process that happens when yeast is added to a sugary solution. The yeast multiplies vigorously, causing a chemical reaction to take place, thus turning the sugar into approximately half alcohol and half carbon dioxide (this produces the bubbles in a sparkling wine). The fermentation has two stages: the first stage will happen in your fermentation bucket and will last for anything up to a week, you will notice this from the froth that develops on the surface of the liquid. The second stage will happen when the liquid has been strained and placed in the demijohn/ fermentation jug. Once the jug has been fitted with

Fitting an air lock to allow carbon dioxide to escape.

an air lock (see below), you will begin to see bubbles being released through the water contained in the air lock. This can take from two months up to a year.

Temperature plays a key role in successful wine making. Yeast kept above 100°F (38°C) will be killed and yeast kept at too low a temperature will be very slow to react. In all of the wine making recipes I suggest putting the fermentation bucket in a warm location—that is to say, a temperature of 70°F (21°C). Once the liquid is placed in the fermenting jug the temperature should be about 65°F (18°C). All finished wine should be stored at about 50°F (10°C). However, you should not get hung up on achieving precise temperatures; a variation of a couple of degrees either way will not hurt.

## Fitting an air lock

When commencing the second stage of fermentation (after the liquid has been strained off the must and placed in the demijohn, or fermentation jug), you will need to fit an air lock. Also known as a fermentation trap or fermentation lock, this is a small plastic device that fits into the center of a large cork, or bung, that fits into the neck of the fermentation jug. The two chambers of the air lock are filled halfway with water; this allows the carbon dioxide to be released while not exposing the wine to any air. The air lock also keeps out the dreaded vinegar fly (commonly called a fruit fly), which, as its name suggests, would turn your wine to vinegar!

## Clearing

If you have been scrupulous with your cleaning of equipment and have not used overboiled fruit, the wine will clear naturally, given time and patience. If, however, you find that it has not cleared after many months, you can speed this up with the use of finings. These are available from any good wine makers' supplier. However, note that their use can upset the chemical balance of the wine. Before you decide to add finings, it may be wise to try one last natural trick: move the wine at the end of the fermentation from a warm place to a cool location (garage or pantry, or larder). As clearing commences, you will notice the solids start to fall to the bottom of the jar, forming what is known as the lees. Over time the wine will become clear from the top down.

Racking wine to get rid of sediment.          Bottling once fermentation has finished.

## Racking/Siphoning

To rack a wine is to siphon it off the lees of the yeast and all the solids that have sunk to the bottom of the demijohn, or fermenting jug, and into another fermenting jug. During the first fermentation in the jug, the wine will look milky and quite unappealing. As the yeast and other solids begin to sink to the bottom of the jug, forming a thick layer there, the wine will start to clear from the top down. Once this has happened, rack the wine into a clean jug.

To rack your wine, you will need to have the jug containing the wine placed higher than the clean, empty jar. Then use the siphoning kit, which will consist of a length of clear hose and a piece of piping. Place the pipe end into the wine halfway into the demijohn and put the end of the hose into your mouth; suck until the wine flows and you get a mouthful of wine (normally a pleasant indication of how the wine will eventually taste); then direct the hose into the neck of the empty jug and fill. As the wine drains out you will have to lower the pipe in the original jug, but you must be careful not to agitate the lees at the bottom. Once all of the liquid has drained out, refit the air lock onto the newly filled jug to proceed with the next fermentation. Note that you may find that fruits, such as plums, that have had boiling water poured on them will be slower to clear.

## Bottling

Once all of the fermentation has ceased, you can either leave it in the fermentation jug or siphon it into bottles. To leave it in the fermentation jug, just remove the cork and air lock and replace these with a rubber bung. This can greatly reduce the number of bottles needed at any one time and the space needed to store the wine. If you do decide to bottle all of the wine, make sure the bottles have been sterilized and that all corks are new, so reducing the possibility of introducing bacteria to your wine. Always use dark green bottles to store red wine, as this will help to preserve its color.

# Equipment

The following is a list of the items you will need to make your own drinks.

**Fermenting bucket** with tight-fitting lid with a capacity of at least 2 U.S. (or U.K.) gallons (7.5–9 liters respectively).

**Funnel**

**White plastic spoon** (do not use a metal spoon, which could have a chemical reaction with the acids and yeasts, or a wooden spoon, which could crack and soften in boiling liquids and harbor bacterial infection).

**Glass bottles:** these can be of the standard plain type that you can buy from wine makers' suppliers or pretty bottles that you have saved from other drinks, etc., but beware of any damage or fragility.

**Ice cube trays:** useful for freezing small batches of a syrup, so that you can use a little at a time. Use white trays, so that you can easily check them for cleanliness.

**Plastic bottles:** any small water bottles can be used for freezing larger amounts of syrups; fill only two-thirds of the bottle—otherwise it will explode in the freezer!

**Sieve (strainer):** This can be made of nylon or metal and should be at least 7 inches (18cm) in diameter; 8 inches (20cm) is better.

**Jelly bag,** or a good-size piece of soft muslin, cheesecloth, or similar fabric.

**Sterilizing tablets** (such as Campden tablets) or powder.

**Demijohns, or fermentation jugs:** these are widely available in various sizes, including some holding several gallons; but for the recipes in this book you will need small ones, holding one U.S. gallon (3.79 liters) or one British gallon (4.55 liters).

**Clear and green glass wine bottles and corks or plastic stoppers**

**Bungs** for demijohns containing a hole for the air lock.

**Clear glass, large, sealable jars:** these are called "mason jars" in the U.S. and Kilner jars in Britain.

**Air locks**

**Strong, long-handled bottle/demijohn brush,** angled so the neck of the demijohn can be cleaned.

**Siphoning hose**

**Large saucepan/stockpot with lid.**

## Basic ingredients

**Campden tablets:** crushed Campden tablets are used to stop the browning of fruit (which occurs, for example, when an apple is cut open) from tainting the finished wine. They are also used for sterilization purposes.

**Citric acid:** this reacts with the yeast to help bring out the flavor of the fruit. Most fruits (though not grapes) naturally provide some acidity, but where this is low, the addition of citric acid will improve the flavor.

**Grape concentrate:** grape concentrate will give the wine added body; for example, white grape concentrate might be added to apple wine, which has a wonderful aroma but is somewhat lacking in body. Red concentrate does the same for red wines, such as raspberry.

**Pectic enzyme:** this additive helps to clear wine. Some fruits, such as plums, are high in pectin, which can make the wine cloudy. The pectic enzyme effectively "eats" all of the pectin in the wine, ensuring a clear result.

**Superfine (caster) sugar:** this is the ingredient that is converted into the alcohol. It dissolves faster than ordinary granulated sugar.

**Vitamin B1 tablets:** this nutrient enables the yeast to continue fermenting until all of the sugar has been converted into either alcohol or carbon dioxide.

**Wine tannin:** this plant-derived substance will improve the flavor of a wine that is a bit unassertive, such as elderflower and some other floral wines. It gives wine its astringency and storing capabilities.

**Wine yeast:** this is the main character in your wine making journey; it will need to be fed (sugar), given nutrients to stay healthy and have longevity (yeast nutrient, vitamin B1), and be exposed to oxygen (but only in the first few days), warmth, and a little acid. The balanced combination of these ingredients will encourage the yeast to reproduce, thus yielding the essential end product: alcohol.

**Yeast nutrient:** as its name suggests, this is a kind of food that assists the yeast to convert sugar into alcohol.

# Troubleshooting

### Oversweet wine

If the wine is too sweet after fermentation is complete, the fermentation may have "stuck," which means that it has stopped before all of the sugar has been converted into alcohol. This could have arisen because there was too much sugar used or because the wine was racked too soon. One way to rectify this is to put the wine back into a sterilized bucket and stir vigorously to allow air back into it; after a couple of days this should get the fermentation process going again. Another remedy is to add a teaspoonful of lemon juice or yeast nutrient to the wine in the jug. Moving the fermentation jug from a cool to a warm location might also do the trick.

### Bland wine

If the wine lacks flavor, this may be caused by a lack of tannins or acid. Try adding a teaspoon of lemon juice or strong black tea, which will help to improve the flavor of the wine.

### Cloudy or hazy wine

If the wine is slow to clear and has finished fermenting, bake a few eggshells until dry, crush them, and add a teaspoonful to the fermentation jug. Leave the wine for a few weeks, by which time it should be clearer. If, however, the wine has stone fruit as its base, such as cherries or plums, which are rich in pectin, use a teaspoonful of pectic enzyme.and place the jar in a warm place for four days. This should do the trick.

### Slow/stuck fermentation

Wine yeasts need a certain amount of vitamins to get a good fermentation going. If, for whatever reason, fermentation gets stuck, a yeast energizer (available from wine makers' suppliers) may be needed. Yeast energizer contains ingredients not found in yeast nutrient. The best way of using it is to dissolve ½ teaspoonful in 1 cup (about 230ml) of the wine, then pour this back into the fermentation jug containing the rest of the wine.

### Fizzy wine

If you find that you have fizzy wine, this is because fermentation has not been completed. If the wine has already been bottled, put it back into the fermentation jug and refit an air lock. If fermentation seems to be stuck or a little slow, follow the advice given above.

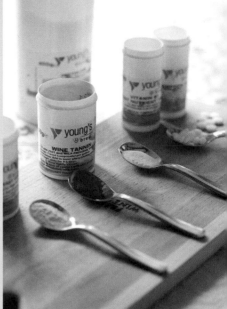

## Troubles to avoid

### Mold forming on top of syrups

This will occur if equipment and bottles have not been properly sterilized. Your only option really is to throw the syrup away; for even if you were to strain out the mold, the syrup would still have a nasty, almost alcoholic taste.

### Oxidization of liqueurs

The only real danger of spoiling a liqueur is exposing it to the air, or more specifically, to oxygen. Oxidization is a process that turns fruit brown, turns complex flavors into bland ones, and turns a good liqueur into a stale one. When a liqueur oxidizes, it turns brown, the sugars break down, and the solids stick together and form a clump at the bottom. So work on the basis that if the liqueur starts to fall apart or change state, you should get rid of it and start again, remembering to keep bottles or jars used tightly sealed.

# Chapter I
# Wines

Preparation: 30 minutes
Cooking: 25 minutes
Makes about 1 gallon (4.5 liters)

INGREDIENTS

7 pounds (3.5kg) apples
7 cups (900g) blackberries
4¼ cups (1kg) superfine (caster)
sugar
4 quarts (4.5 liters) water
1 vitamin B1 tablet (450mg)
1 teaspoon wine yeast
1 teaspoon yeast nutrient
1 teaspoon pectic enzyme
4 quarts (4.5 liters) water
½ cup (150ml) grape concentrate

# Blackberry & apple wine

This recipe produces a lovely sweet wine with a beautiful color.
It's an excellent way to use a glut of blackberries or apples.
Serve the wine with strong cheese and rustic bread.

1. Chop the apples into chunks (no need to peel or core them),
blitz them in a blender, and set aside. Put the berries in a sterilized
fermenting bucket (see page 12).

2. Put the sugar into a large pan, cover slightly with some of
the water, and bring to a boil. (Be very careful, as this will be
extremely hot.)

3. Pour the boiling sugar syrup over the blackberries and stir well,
making sure all of the berries are reduced to a pulp. Add the apple
pulp to the berries and stir in. Allow to cool for 1 hour.

4. In another pan, heat 1½ quarts (1.7 liters) of the water to
lukewarm, then dissolve the vitamin B1 tablet in it. Allow to cool.

5. Add the vitamin solution to the bucket, along with the yeast,
yeast nutrient, pectic enzyme, and grape concentrate. Allow the
mixture to ferment for 5 days.

6. After the 5 days, strain through a fine sieve lined with fine
muslin or cheesecloth (see page 12) and pour into a demijohn.

7. Fill the demijohn up to the neck with cold water, and fit an air
lock (see page 14).

8. When the wine is clear, siphon it off (see page 15) into sterilized
bottles and cork (see page 13). Store it in a cool, dark place. It will
be ready for drinking in 6 months.

## Blackberry wine
Simply omit the apples and replace them with the
same quantity of blackberries as the apples. So
you would need a total of 9¾ pounds (4.4kg)
of blackberries.

# Rose petal & peach wine

Preparation: 30 minutes
Cooking: 30 minutes
Makes about 1 gallon (4.5 liters)

### INGREDIENTS

2 pounds (1.1kg) peaches (6 large)
8 1/2 cups (100g) rose petals
6 cups (1.35kg) superfine (caster)
sugar
4 quarts (4.5 liters) water (total)
1 teaspoon citric acid
1 cup (285ml) strong tea
1 teaspoon wine yeast
1 teaspoon yeast nutrient

This is a wonderfully fragrant medium wine. If possible, use fresh petals from the garden (provided they've not been sprayed with any chemicals) or purchase dried rose petals from a wine-making supplier. Enjoy this wine with barbecued trout, stuffed with rose petals or with fruit skewers cooked on a griddle, served with a dip made of sour cream (or crème fraîche) and chopped mint.

1. Pit (but do not peel) the peaches. Rinse the rose petals, if using fresh ones. Put the peaches, rose petals, and sugar in a sterilized (see page 12) fermenting bucket, placed in a warm place.

2. Boil the water in a large pan. Pour it over the fruit and sugar and stir, making sure that all the sugar has dissolved.

3. Allow to cool to 70°F (21°C) (see page 14), then add the citric acid, tea, yeast, and yeast nutrient. Stir thoroughly.

4. Secure the lid tightly on the bucket and leave for a week, stirring daily.

5. After the 7 days, strain the contents (see page 12). Pour into a sterilized demijohn and fit an air lock (see page 14).

6. Once the fermentation has ceased, rack the liquid (see page 15) into another sterilized demijohn, placed in a cooler location, and allow it to clear.

7. Siphon the wine (see page 15) into sterilized bottles and cork (see page 13). Store the bottles in a cool, dark place. Leave for 6 months, then taste. If the wine is not to your liking, recork and try it after another month. Repeat as necessary.

## Peach wine

If you don't have many rose petals, you can omit them and just use peaches.

# Summer wine

Preparation: 30 minutes
Cooking: 20 minutes
Makes about 4³/₄ quarts (4.5 liters)

## INGREDIENTS

6 cups (650g) strawberries, hulled

4 cups (450g) raspberries

2 cups (450g) gooseberries

1¹/₂ cups (250g) red or white
currants

4¹/₂ cups (1kg) superfine (caster)
sugar

4 quarts (4.5 liters) water

1 teaspoon pectic enzyme

1 teaspoon wine yeast

1 teaspoon yeast nutrient

1 crushed Campden tablet

### Now try this

Serve this wine chilled, with

a rich chocolate dessert,

such as a dark chocolate and

almond soufflé. Rosé wine

is in a class of its own, as it

has the ability to be paired

with most food.

This recipe produces a beautiful pale rosé, medium wine. Be sure to keep it stored in a dark place to preserve its color. The gooseberries should be the green European kind; if you can't get them, you might substitute 3¹/₂ cups (450g) blueberries. This will produce a more intense color.

1. Put all fruit in a sterilized fermenting bucket (see page 12). Add the sugar.

2. Put 3¹/₄ quarts (3.4 liters) of water in a large pan and bring to a boil. Pour the water over the fruit. Mash the fruit with a potato masher to reduce it to a pulp and stir, making sure that all the sugar has dissolved.

3. Allow the liquid to cool to 70°F (21°C) and add the pectic enzyme. Secure the lid on the bucket, place it in a warm location, and leave it for 24 hours.

4. Add the yeast and yeast nutrient and stir well. Replace the lid and allow the contents to ferment for another week, stirring daily.

5. Strain the must (see page 12) and pour the wine into a sterilized demijohn.

6. Boil the remaining water, allow it to cool, and pour it into the demijohn. Fit an air lock (see page 14).

7. When the fermentation has finished, rack the wine (see page 15) and allow it to clear. Pour it into sterilized bottles and cork (see page 13). Store the wine in a cool, dark place and leave it for 6 months before drinking.

# Elderflower wine

When the first flush of elderflowers emerges, this is the time to start your wine-making year. The flowers don't last long, so I like to make the most of this free bounty in as many drinks as possible. This recipe makes a beautiful dry wine. Serve it with chicken roasted with garlic, new potatoes, and a garden salad, perhaps using a dressing containing Elderflower Syrup (see page 60).

Preparation: 30 minutes

Cooking: 40 minutes

Makes about 1 gallon (4.5 liters)

### INGREDIENTS

10 heads of elderflower (see page 11)

2 cups (300g) raisins

4 quarts (4.5 liters) water

6½ cups (1.5kg) superfine (caster) sugar

3 lemons, juice only

1 teaspoon wine yeast

1 teaspoon yeast nutrient

1 teaspoon grape tannin

1. Prepare the elderflowers (see page 11) and put them in a sterilized fermenting bucket located in a warm place (see page 12). Chop the raisins roughly.

2. Pour the water into a large pan and bring it to a boil. Pour it over the elderflower heads. Add the raisins, sugar, and lemon juice, and give it a stir.

3. Allow the mixture to cool to 70°F (21°C), then add the yeast, yeast nutrient, and grape tannin. Secure the lid tightly on the bucket and let the wine ferment for 5 days.

4. Strain the wine through a piece of fine muslin or cheesecloth (see page 12). Pour it into a sterilized demijohn, and fit an air lock (see page 14). Leave to ferment until it has cleared.

5. Siphon the wine off the deposit (see page 15) into another sterilized demijohn and fit an air lock. Leave it for 2 months.

6. Siphon off the wine again. Pour into sterilized bottles, cork (see page 13), and store in a cool, dark place.

# Sparkling elderflower wine

Preparation: 30 minutes

Cooking: 30 minutes

Makes about 1 gallon (4.5 liters)

INGREDIENTS

20 heads elderflower (see page 11)

4 unwaxed lemons, juice and zest

3 cups (700g) superfine (caster) sugar

5¼ quarts (6 liters) water

2 tablespoons white wine vinegar

1 teaspoon wine yeast or Champagne yeast

1 teaspoon yeast nutrient

Here is another great way to use up elderflowers. But beware: this drink has a tendency to explode; so use bottles with strong lids, such as swing-top beer bottles or plastic bottles. This would make a delightful drink for a christening or a summer wedding at home.

1. Put the elderflowers in a sterilized fermenting bucket (you won't need the lid) in a cool, airy location (see page 12). Add the lemon juice and zest and the sugar.

2. Pour 3½ quarts (4 liters) of the water into a large pan and bring to a boil. Pour it over the ingredients in the bucket and add the vinegar. Stir to make sure all the sugar has dissolved.

3. Add the remaining water and allow the contents to cool to 70°F (21°C). Add the yeast and yeast nutrient. Cover the bucket with a piece of fine muslin or cheesecloth and let it ferment for 4 days.

4. Strain the wine through a sieve lined with fine muslin or cheesecloth (see page 12) and pour it into sterilized bottles. Use strong swing-lid or plastic bottles, which will withstand the pressure from the wine.

5. Store the wine in a cool, dark place. It will be ready to drink after a week and should keep for 4 months.

# Gooseberry wine

Preparation: 30 minutes
Cooking: not required
Makes about 1 gallon (4.5 liters)

INGREDIENTS
·····················

6 pounds (2.7kg) gooseberries
4 quarts (4.5 liters) water
1 teaspoon pectic enzyme
5¹/₂ cups (1.25kg) superfine (caster) sugar
1 teaspoon wine yeast
1 teaspoon yeast nutrient

This recipe produces a dry wine. Ideally it should be made with green, European gooseberries, which are growing in popularity in the United States. This wine is a good partner for a dish of large pork meatballs with tomato and herb sauce, served with the pasta of your choice.

1. Remove the stem and blossom end of the gooseberries and put them in a sterilized fermenting bucket (see page 12). Crush them by hand with a potato masher until they have turned to a pulp.

2. Pour the water on top and add the pectic enzyme. Secure the lid on the bucket. Leave it to ferment for 3 days, giving it a stir daily.

3. Strain the liquid through a sieve lined with fine muslin or cheesecloth (see page 12). Add the sugar and stir until it has dissolved. Add the yeast and yeast nutrient.

4. Pour the liquid into a sterilized demijohn and fit an air lock (see page 14). Leave it to ferment until all the bubbling has ceased.

5. Siphon off the wine (see page 15) and leave it to mature—that is, develop its flavor—for 6 months.

6. Siphon off the wine again and pour it into sterilized bottles. Store it in a cool, dark place and leave it for a year before drinking.

# Raspberry wine

Preparation: 30 minutes
Cooking: 30 minutes
Makes about 1 gallon (4.5 liters)

### INGREDIENTS

4 pounds (1.8kg) raspberries

4 quarts (4.5 liters) water

1 teaspoon pectic enzyme

6½ cups (1.5kg) superfine (caster) sugar

1¼ cups (300ml) red grape concentrate

1 teaspoon wine yeast

1 teaspoon yeast nutrient

If you can resist the temptation to eat the raspberries, before using them in this recipe, you'll be rewarded with a lovely sweet wine. Try serving it with a delicious homemade raspberry cheesecake.

1. Put the raspberries into a sterilized fermenting bucket (see page 12). Put the water in a large pan and bring to a boil. Then allow it to cool for 1 hour. Pour it over the raspberries and add the pectic enzyme.

2. Mash the fruit well with a potato masher, then secure the lid on the bucket. Leave it to ferment for 4 days, stirring once a day.

3. Strain the liquid through a double thickness of fine muslin or cheesecloth (see page 12).

4. Put the sugar and the grape concentrate in another sterilized fermenting bucket, located in a warm place, and pour the raspberry liquid on top. Stir well to make sure all the sugar has dissolved. Add the yeast and yeast nutrient and stir well. Secure the lid on the bucket and leave it for another 24 hours.

5. Pour the liquid into a sterilized demijohn. Fit an air lock (see page 14). Leave the wine to ferment until it clears.

6. Siphon the wine into sterilized bottles (see page 15) and cork (see page 13). Store it in a cool, dark place. It should be ready for drinking in 6 months.

## Loganberry or Tayberry wine

Instead of raspberries, you could make the wine from loganberries, boysenberries, or tayberries, using the same weight of fruit.

# Elderberry wine

Preparation: 40 minutes

Cooking: 25 minutes

Makes about 1 gallon (4.5 liters)

INGREDIENTS
.................

10 cups (1.5kg) elderberries
(stripped from stems)

4 quarts (4.5 liters) water

1 teaspoon wine yeast

1 teaspoon yeast nutrient

1 teaspoon citric acid

6½ cups (1.5kg) superfine (caster)
sugar

After you've made your Elderflower Wine (see page 26), you can use the berries from this versatile plant to make this fantastic wine. This wine goes beautifully with lamb; serve it with chops, roast lamb, or lamb casserole. You could add a little of the wine to the cooking juices for a rich gravy.

1. Put the berries in a sterilized fermenting bucket and crush them using a potato masher.

2. Put the water in a large pan and bring it to a boil. Pour it over the berries. Wait for the mixture to cool down to 70°F (21°C), then add the yeast, yeast nutrient, and citric acid.

3. Cover the bucket tightly with the lid and leave it to ferment for 4 days, stirring daily.

4. Put the sugar in a second sterilized fermenting bucket. Strain the liquid through a fine sieve (see page 12) then pour it onto the sugar.

5. Pour the liquid into a dark-colored demijohn, but not right up to the neck. Discard any left over. Place a wad of absorbent cotton (cotton wool) in the neck and leave to ferment. This first fermentation will be quite vigorous.

6. Once the fermentation has subsided, fill the demijohn up to the neck with more water and fit an air lock (see page 14). Leave it until the fermentation has subsided.

7. Siphon off the wine (see page 15) into dark, sterilized bottles, and cork (see page 13). Store the wine in a cool, dark place for at least 6 months.

## Sloe wine
Try using sloes instead of elderberries, or a mixture of the two.

# Blueberry wine

Preparation: 30 minutes
Cooking: 40 minutes
Makes about 1 gallon (4.5 liters)

### INGREDIENTS

3¼ pounds (1.5kg) fresh or frozen blueberries

4 quarts (4.5 liters) water

1 Campden tablet

1 cup (250ml) red grape concentrate

1 teaspoon wine yeast

1 teaspoon yeast nutrient

1 teaspoon pectic enzyme

4½ cups (1kg) superfine (caster) sugar

If blueberries are not in season, you could use frozen ones for this recipe, which makes a lovely red wine. To vary the taste, you could try using different kinds of wine yeast, such as a Bordeaux. Use a little of this wine to enrich the gravy for a roasted cut of meat, such as beef, pork, duck, or game.

**1.** Put the blueberries in a sterilized fermenting bucket (see page 12), placed in a warm location. Boil the water in a large pan, then pour it into the bucket. Allow the contents to cool, then mash the blueberries with a potato masher.

**2.** Crush the Campden tablet and add it to the bucket, along with the grape concentrate, yeast, yeast nutrient, pectic enzyme, and half the sugar. Stir well. Secure the lid on the bucket. Leave it for 4 days, giving the mixture a stir once a day.

**3.** Strain the liquid off the pulp (see page 12) into a sterilized demijohn. Add the remaining sugar. Fit an air lock (see page 14).

**4.** Leave the wine to finish fermenting and become clear. Pour it into sterilized green bottles. Store the wine in a cool, dark place; it should be ready for drinking in 6 months.

# Ginger wine

Preparation: 30 minutes
Cooking: 1½ hours
Makes about 1 gallon (4.5 liters)

### INGREDIENTS

11 ounces (310g) gingerroot

3 unwaxed lemons, juice and zest

1 orange, juice and zest

¼ cup (30g) cloves

4 quarts (4.5 liters) water

3½ cups (700g) brown crystal (demerara) sugar

3½ cups (700g) loosely packed dark brown sugar

1 teaspoon yeast nutrient

1 teaspoon wine yeast

This is a lovely wine. Save it for a winter's evening when you're curled up in front of a fire. Drink it by itself, with just some good company.

1. Crush the ginger roughly using a pestle and mortar. Place it in a muslin (cheesecloth) bag , along with the lemon and orange zest and the cloves.

2. Put the water in a large pan and bring to a boil. Reduce to a simmer and drop in the muslin bag. Leave it to simmer for 1 hour, then remove the bag.

3. Put all of the sugar in a sterilized fermenting bucket (see page 12), placed in a warm location. Pour in the liquid and stir until all the sugar has dissolved. Add the citrus juice and the yeast nutrient.

4. Allow the liquid to cool down to 70°F (21°C), then add the yeast. Cover tightly with the lid and leave for 4 days.

5. Stir the mixture, pour it into a sterilized demijohn, and fit an air lock (see page 14). Leave the wine to ferment until it clears.

6. Siphon the wine (see page 15) into a fresh sterilized demijohn and fit an air lock.

7. When the wine has completely cleared and has thrown a second deposit (see page 14), fermentation has stopped.

8. Siphon the wine into sterilized bottles (see page 15), cork (see page 13), and store in a cool, dark place for 6 months before drinking.

# Rose wine

Preparation: 25 minutes
Cooking: 30 minutes
Makes about 1 gallon (4.5 liters)

### INGREDIENTS

4 quarts (4.5 liters) water

9 cups (150g) rose petals

5½ cups (1.25kg) superfine (caster) sugar

2 teaspoons citric acid

1⅛ cups (280ml) grape concentrate

1 teaspoon wine yeast

1 teaspoon yeast nutrient

Rose petals are great for making wine. I would always urge you to use dried petals, as these produce a better taste, but fresh ones are fine if you've got an abundance of them that you'd prefer not to throw on the compost heap. Try serving this wine with barbecued fish or alongside cheese and crusty bread.

1. Put the water into a large pan and bring to a boil. Add the rose petals, sugar, citric acid, and grape concentrate. Stir well. Remove from the heat.

2. Allow to cool to about 70°F (21°C), then add the yeast and yeast nutrient.

3. Pour the contents of the pan into a sterilized fermenting bucket (see page 12). Cover it tightly with the lid. Leave the mixture to ferment for a week, giving it a stir once a day.

4. Strain the liquid (see page 12) and pour it into a sterilized demijohn. Fit an air lock (see page 14). Leave to ferment until the wine is clear.

5. Pour the wine into sterilized bottles and cork (see page 13). Store the wine in a cool, dark place. It should be ready to drink after 6 months.

# Fig & rose hip wine

This recipe will produce a fantastic medium-sweet wine. Use dried figs, as they not only are cheaper than fresh ones but also produce a better result. Serve this wine chilled. It goes surprisingly well with chili con carne. This wine can take quite a while to clear, so you may need to siphon it (see page 15) several times. If this happens, pour in clear apple juice until the demijohn is filled to the neck and the correct level of liquid is maintained.

1. Chop the figs roughly and put them in a sterilized fermenting bucket (see page 12) along with the rose hips.

2. Boil 2½ quarts (2.5 liters) of the water and pour it into the bucket. Leave the mixture to soak overnight.

3. Put the sugar and 2 cups (500ml) of water in a pan and bring to a boil. Stir until the sugar has dissolved. Pour this syrup into the bucket.

4. Add the pectic enzyme, citric acid, and yeast nutrient. Allow to cool to 70°F (21°C) then add the yeast. Secure the lid on the bucket and place in a warm location; leave it for 1 week, stirring daily.

5. Strain the liquid through a sieve (see page 12), then pour it into a sterilized demijohn. Fit an air lock (see page 14). Leave to ferment.

6. When all fermentation has ceased and the wine begins to clear, transfer the demijohn to a cool place. When the sediment starts to form, siphon it off (see page 15) into another sterilized demijohn and add a crushed Campden tablet.

7. Siphon the wine into sterilized bottles and cork (see page 13). Store in a cool, dark place for at least 6 months before tasting.

Preparation: 30 minutes
Cooking: 20 minutes
Makes about 1 gallon (4.5 liters)

INGREDIENTS

3 cups (450g) dried figs
2 cups (225g) rose hips
1 gallon (4.5 liters) water
3 cups (675g) superfine (caster) sugar
1 teaspoon pectic enzyme
1 teaspoon citric acid
1 teaspoon yeast nutrient
1 teaspoon wine yeast
1 Campden tablet

# Plum wine

This recipe will produce a lovely sweet wine. I use Victoria plums, which are excellent and very plentiful in Britain; choose the best variety available in your area. Serve this wine with cheese, crackers, and chutney.

Preparation: 20 minutes
Cooking: 30 minutes
Makes about 1 gallon (4.5 liters)

INGREDIENTS

6 pounds (2.7kg) plums
4 quarts (4.5 liters) water
1 teaspoon pectic acid
6¹/₂ cups (1.5kg) superfine (caster) sugar
1 teaspoon wine yeast
1 teaspoon yeast nutrient

I. Cut the plums in half and remove the pits. Place them in a sterilized fermenting bucket (see page 12) and crush them with a potato masher.

2. Put half the water in a large pan and bring to a boil. Pour the boiling water over the plums. Leave the mixture, covered, for 5 hours, then add the rest of the water (cold). Add the pectic enzyme and leave for another 2 days.

3. Strain the liquid through a fine sieve (see page 12), put it in a large pan, and bring to a boil.

4. Put the sugar in the fermenting bucket and pour the boiling juice over the top. Stir it well, making sure all the sugar has dissolved.

5. Allow the mixture to cool to 70°F (21°C), then add the yeast and yeast nutrient.

6. Sterilize a funnel and pour the liquid through it into a sterilized demijohn. Fit an air lock (see page 14).

7. When the wine begins to clear, siphon it off (see page 15) into another sterilized demijohn. Refit an air lock and allow to continue fermenting.

8. When all fermentation has finished, siphon the wine off into sterilized bottles. Store in a cool, dark place. It should be ready for drinking in 6 months.

## Damson wine

If damsons (also called damson plums) are available in your area, you could use these for this wine.

# Prune wine

Preparation: 30 minutes
Cooking: 10 minutes
Makes about 1 gallon (4.5 liters)

### INGREDIENTS

2 pounds (1kg) prunes

4 quarts (4.5 liters) water

1 teaspoon pectic enzyme

1 Campden tablet

6½ cups (1.5kg) superfine (caster) sugar

½ cup (150ml) red grape concentrate

1 teaspoon red wine yeast

1 teaspoon yeast nutrient

This is an excellent wine to make during the winter months, when fruits from the garden and the countryside have gone and your passion for wine making is as strong as ever. The recipe produces a sweet wine—the perfect accompaniment to a rich dessert.

1. Chop the prunes coarsely and put them into a sterilized fermenting bucket (see page 12) placed in a warm location. Boil half the water and pour it over them. Cover the bucket with its lid, and leave it for 24 hours.

2. Add the rest of the water and the pectic enzyme. Secure the lid on the bucket. Leave it for 10 days, stirring it daily.

3. Strain the liquid through a sieve (see page 12). Put the pulp in a large piece of fine muslin or cheesecloth and squeeze the remaining juice from it. Return all the juice to the bucket. Crush the Campden tablet and add it, along with the sugar and grape concentrate to the bucket. Stir until all the sugar has dissolved. Add the yeast and yeast nutrient.

4. Leave the wine to ferment in the bucket for another 10 days, stirring it daily.

5. Strain the liquid again, pour it into a sterilized demijohn, and fit an air lock (see page 14).

6. Once the wine has cleared, siphon it (see page 15) into sterilized green bottles. Store the wine in a cool, dark place and leave it for 6 months before trying.

# Cherry wine

Preparation: 20 minutes
Cooking: 25 minutes
Makes about 1 gallon (4.5 liters)

INGREDIENTS

6 pounds (2.7kg) black cherries
4 quarts (4.5 liters) water
9 cups (2kg) superfine (caster) sugar
1 teaspoon citric acid
1 teaspoon wine yeast
1 teaspoon yeast nutrient

Try to use black cherries for this sweet wine, but if you are picking your own, use whatever you've got—if the birds don't get to them first! Serve this dessert wine with a lovely homemade tiramisu for a glamorous end to a dinner party.

1. Remove the stalks from the cherries and put them in a sterilized fermenting bucket (see page 12). Crush the cherries with your hands (wearing rubber gloves, if you like, to avoid stains; there is no need to remove the pits).

2. Bring the water to a boil, then pour it over the cherries. Cover the bucket tightly with the lid and leave it for 48 hours.

3. Strain the liquid through a sieve (see page 12). Put it in a pan and bring to the boil. Put the sugar in the bucket (positioned in a warm place) and pour the boiling juice on top. Stir until all the sugar has dissolved.

4. Allow the mixture to cool for 1 hour, then stir in the citric acid, yeast, and yeast nutrient. Replace the cover on the bucket and allow to ferment for 2 weeks.

5. Pour the wine into a sterilized demijohn and fit an air lock (see page 14).

6. When the wine is clear, siphon it off (see page 15) into sterilized bottles. Store it in a cool, dark place. It should be ready for drinking in 6 months.

# Apple wine

Preparation: 30 minutes

Cooking: 30 minutes

Makes about 1 gallon (4.5 liters)

### INGREDIENTS

6 pounds (2.7kg) apples

4 quarts (4.5 liters) water

4¼ cups (1kg) superfine (caster) sugar

1 teaspoon citric acid

1 teaspoon wine yeast

1 teaspoon yeast nutrient

⅝ cups (150ml) white grape concentrate

This recipe will produce a beautiful, dry wine that tastes fantastic when paired with fish or pork dishes. Be sure to make use of any windfalls that you can find, a mix of different varieties is perfect.

1. Wash the apples and roughly chop into chunks, leaving on the skin and brown patches. Put the fruit into a large pan with the water and bring to a boil. Simmer for a further 15 minutes.

2. Put the apples and water into a sterilized fermenting bucket (see page 12) and add the sugar and citric acid. Stir to make sure that all of the sugar has dissolved.

3. Allow the liquid to cool to 70°F (21°C), then add the yeast, yeast nutrient, and concentrate. Put the lid securely on the bucket and leave the wine in a warm place for 24 hours.

4. Pour the liquid into a sterilized fermenting jar (do not strain at this stage) and fit an air lock (see page 14). Leave to ferment for 4 more weeks.

5. Siphon the wine off (see page 15) into another sterilized demijohn, refit the air lock, and leave to ferment.

6. Once all the bubbling has ceased, siphon off the wine into bottles, cork (see page 13), and leave the wine in a cool dark place to mature for at least 6 months.

## Pear wine or Apple & Elderflower wine

For a delicious pear wine, simply replace the apples with 6 pounds (2.7kg) of pears, or try a mixture of the two for a real taste of the orchard.

Another excellent addition to this recipe is that of elderflower. Use around 12 good-sized heads to give that extra bit of flavor to the wine.

# Quince wine

Preparation: 40 minutes
Cooking: 15 minutes
Makes about 1 gallon (4.5 liters)

### INGREDIENTS

20 ripe quinces

4 quarts (4.5 liters) water

4½ cups (1kg) superfine (caster) sugar

2 unwaxed lemons, juice and zest

1 Campden tablet

1 teaspoon pectic enzyme

1½ cups (350ml) freshly squeezed orange juice

1 teaspoon Champagne yeast

1 teaspoon yeast nutrient

Quinces can be hard to find, so if you do manage to discover some, take advantage of the opportunity to make this lovely wine. It will take a while to clear, but persevere; it is well worth the wait. Do not be tempted to boil the pulp any longer than 10 minutes, as overboiling will produce a cloudy effect. Serve this wine with white fish or a lobster salad.

1. Grate the quinces and put them in a pan with just enough of the water to cover the pulp. Bring the mixture to a boil and let boil for just 10 minutes. Then remove from the heat and allow to cool.

2. Strain the liquid through a piece of fine muslin or cheesecloth (see page 12) into a sterilized fermenting bucket (see page 12) placed in a warm location.

3. Add the sugar and the lemon juice and zest. Crush the Campden tablet and add it to the bucket, along with the pectic enzyme. Secure the lid on the bucket and leave it for 24 hours.

4. Add the orange juice, Champagne yeast, and yeast nutrient. Add the rest of the water. Cover the bucket again and leave it for 3 days, stirring once a day.

5. Pour the liquid into a sterilized demijohn and fit an air lock (see page 14).

6. When the wine has finished fermenting and is clear (you may need to rack it off into other sterilized demijohns a few times to get it to clear completely), siphon it (see page 15) into sterilized bottles and store in a cool, dark place. Leave it for at least 6 months before trying.

# Strawberry wine

I usually get the strawberries for this wine from a pick-your-own fruit farm—partly because it's a relatively inexpensive way to obtain the large amount needed and partly because it's a good excuse to get out and enjoy the summer weather. This recipe produces a medium-sweet wine. As with any pairing of wine with food, it should be served with food that is less sweet than it is. It would go well with salmon or shellfish or with a platter of cold meats and some rustic bread. Another good way to use this wine is to make a strawberry wine granita.

Preparation: 30 minutes
Cooking: not required
Makes about 1 gallon (4.5 liters)

### INGREDIENTS

4 pounds (2kg) strawberries, hulled
6 1/2 cups (1.5kg) superfine (caster) sugar
4 quarts (4.5 liters) water
1 teaspoon citric acid
1/2 teaspoon grape tannin
1 teaspoon wine yeast
1 teaspoon yeast nutrient

1. Put the strawberries in a sterilized fermenting bucket (see page 12) and mash them with a potato masher.

2. Add the sugar and 2 quarts (2 liters) of the water, and mix well. Secure the lid on the bucket and leave it for 36 hours.

3. Strain the liquid (see page 12) and pour it into a sterilized demijohn. Add another quart (liter) of water to the pulp remaining in the bucket, mix well, and strain again. Add this liquid to the first batch in the demijohn.

4. Add the citric acid, grape tannin, yeast, and yeast nutrient. Pour in the remaining water, stir thoroughly, and fit an air lock (see page 14).

5. Leave the wine to ferment until it clears, then siphon it off (see page 15) into sterilized bottles, and cork (see page 13). Store it in a cool, dark place. Taste the wine after 6 months; if it is not to your taste, leave it for another month and try it again. Repeat if necessary.

# Pineapple wine

Preparation: 20 minutes
Cooking: 40 minutes
Makes about 1 gallon (4.5 liters)

### INGREDIENTS

4 large pineapples

4 quarts (4.5 liters) water

7$^{1}/_{2}$ cups (1.75kg) superfine (caster)
sugar

1 teaspoon citric acid

1 teaspoon wine yeast

1 teaspoon yeast nutrient

1 Campden tablet

1 stabilizing tablet

Since pineapples are relatively easy to get hold of at any time of the year, you can make this wine whenever you like. The recipe produces a sweet, light wine, which is perfect served chilled with a light summer dessert.

1. Remove the top and bottom of each pineapple. Slice them and put them in a large pan, along with 1$^{1}/_{2}$ quarts (1.5 liters) water (or enough to cover). Bring to a boil, then simmer for 25 minutes. Remove from the heat.

2. Put the sugar into a sterilized fermenting bucket (see page 12), placed in a warm location. Strain the liquid from the pan into the bucket (see page 12). Add the remaining water and the citric acid. Stir thoroughly, making sure all the sugar has dissolved.

3. Leave the contents to cool to 70°F (21°C), then add the yeast and yeast nutrient. Secure the lid on the bucket and leave to ferment for 1 week, stirring the contents once a day.

4. Pour the liquid into a sterilized demijohn and fit an air lock (see page 14).

5. Leave until the wine starts to clear and has formed a substantial sediment (see page 15).

6. Siphon off (see page 15) into a fresh, sterilized demijohn. Add a crushed Campden tablet and a stabilizing tablet.

7. When the wine has thrown a fresh sediment, siphon it into sterilized bottles and cork it. Store it in a cool, dark place. Leave it for 6 months before drinking.

# Rhubarb wine

I like to force one of my rhubarb crowns to get some really tender stems specifically for wine making. However, store-bought rhubarb is fine. Always use the dry-sugar method described below, as this will keep the finished wine light. The recipe produces a medium wine. Serve it with a large platter of cured meats and a crisp salad.

Preparation: 20 minutes

Cooking: not required

Makes about 1 gallon (4.5 liters)

INGREDIENTS

3 pounds (1.4kg) rhubarb

6¼ cups (1.4kg) superfine (caster) sugar

4 quarts (4.5 liters) water

1 teaspoon wine yeast

1 teaspoon yeast nutrient

1. Remove the leaves and the bottom edges of the rhubarb stems and slice them thinly. Put the rhubarb in a sterilized fermenting bucket (see page 12) and cover with the sugar.

2. Secure the lid on the bucket and leave it until most of the sugar has dissolved (which will take about 36 hours).

3. Strain the pulp through a sieve (see page 12), straight through a funnel into a sterilized demijohn, positioned in a warm place.

4. Put the pulp back into the bucket, add some water (enough just to cover the pulp), and strain again.

5. Using a little more water, rinse all remaining sugar into the rhubarb liquid. Fill up the demijohn with the rest of the measured water. Add the yeast and the yeast nutrient. Fit an air lock (see page 14).

6. When fermentation is finished—when the wine is clear—pour the wine into sterilized bottles and cork (see page 13). Store it in a cool, dark place. It should be ready for drinking in about 6 months.

# Apricot wine

Preparation: 30 minutes
Cooking: 30 minutes
Makes about 1 gallon (4.5 liters)

## INGREDIENTS

2¼ pounds (1kg) apricots

4 quarts (4.5 liters) water

6½ cups (1.5kg) superfine (caster)
sugar

1 teaspoon yeast nutrient

1 teaspoon wine yeast

1 teaspoon pectic enzyme

1 teaspoon citric acid

This recipe produces a sweet wine. If you cannot get enough fresh apricots, you can substitute dried ones. Just soak them for 12 hours before using. Serve this dessert wine with a delicious apricot tarte Tatin, perhaps topped with a little whipped cream.

1. Halve the apricots and remove the pits. Put them in a large pan with the water, bring to a boil, and simmer for 10 minutes.

2. Strain off the liquid into a sterilized fermenting bucket (see page 12). Add the sugar, yeast nutrient, and pectic enzyme. Stir, making sure all the sugar has dissolved.

3. Leave to cool to approximately 70°F (21°C), then add the citric acid and yeast. Put the lid on the bucket and leave to ferment for 4 days, stirring daily.

4. Pour the wine into a sterilized demijohn and fit an air lock (see page 14).

5. When fermentation has stopped, siphon the wine off (see page 15) into sterilized bottles and cork (see page 13). Store in a cool, dark place for 4 months before tasting. If it is not to your taste, recork and try again after a couple of months.

# Black currant wine

Preparation: 30 minutes
Cooking: 30 minutes
Makes about 1 gallon (4.5 liters)

INGREDIENTS
...........................

3¹/₄ pounds (1.5kg) black currants
8 cups (1.75kg) superfine (caster) sugar
4 quarts (4.5 liters) water
1 teaspoon pectic enzyme
1 teaspoon wine yeast
1 teaspoon yeast nutrient

Black currants with their fruity, sharp taste mean a bottle of this wine never stays long in the store cupboard once a batch is ready to drink. The recipe produces a medium wine. Serve it with homemade lasagne and garlic bruschetta.

1. Strip the currants from their stems and put them in a sterilized fermenting bucket (see page 12).

2. Put the sugar and water in a large pan and bring to a boil. Pour the syrup over the currants.

3. Allow to cool to 70°F (21°C), then add the pectic enzyme. Cover with the lid, place the bucket in a warm place, and leave for 24 hours.

4. Add the yeast and yeast nutrient, cover again, and leave for another 5 days.

5. Strain the wine (see page 12) and pour into a sterilized demijohn. Fit an air lock (see page 14).

6. When the fermentation has stopped and the wine has cleared, siphon (see page 15) it into sterilized bottles and cork (see page 13). Store the wine in a cool, dark place and leave it for 3 months before tasting.

## Red currant wine
If black currants aren't available simply replace them with the same quantity of red or white currants, or try a mix of the two.

# Grapefruit wine

Preparation: 40 minutes

Cooking: not required

Makes about 1 gallon (4.5 liters)

## INGREDIENTS

7 large grapefruit, zest and juice
(see Note)

2 cups (500ml) white grape
concentrate

4 quarts (4.5 liters) water

1 crushed Campden tablet

1 teaspoon wine yeast

1 teaspoon yeast nutrient

$5^1/_2$ cups (1.25kg) superfine (caster)
sugar

Note:
Wash the grapefruit thoroughly,
using a nail brush or similar to
get into all the little holes.
Allow them to dry completely
before removing the zest, which
may take some time.

This recipe makes an astonishingly good dry white wine—
every bit as good as a store-bought wine. It goes especially
well with fish or boiled shrimp.

1. Put the grapefruit juice and zest, the grape concentrate, the
water, and the Campden tablet in a sterilized fermenting bucket
(see page 12) located in a warm place. Cover with the lid and
leave for 24 hours.

2. Add the yeast and yeast nutrient and refit the lid; leave for
a week, stirring once a day.

3. Strain the liquid through a sieve lined with fine muslin or
cheesecloth (see page 12). Pour it back into the bucket and add
the sugar, stirring well to make sure all the sugar has dissolved.

4. Pour the liquid into a sterilized demijohn and fit an air lock
(see page 14).

5. When the wine has finished fermenting and has cleared,
siphon it (see page 15) into sterilized bottles and cork (see
page 13).

# Orange wine

This recipe produces a medium wine with a wonderful aroma. Try serving it with a wonderfully spicy curry or a Moroccan lamb tagine.

**I.** Put the orange zest in a sterilized fermenting bucket (see page 12), placed in a warm location. Boil I quart (I liter) of water and pour it onto the zest. Leave, covered, for 24 hours.

**2.** Strain the liquid through a sieve and pour it back into the bucket. (Discard the zest.) Add 3 more quarts (3.5 liters) water to the bucket.

**3.** Add the sugar to the bucket and stir until all of it has dissolved. Add the yeast, yeast nutrient, and pectic enzyme to the orange juice and stir until mixed well. Add the juice mixture to the bucket and stir well. Secure the lid and leave to ferment for 4–5 days.

**4.** Pour the liquid into a sterilized demijohn and fit an air lock (see page 14).

**5.** After the wine has cleared, siphon it (see page 15) into another sterilized demijohn and refit the air lock.

**6.** After another 3 months the fermenting should be complete. Pour the wine into sterilized bottles and store in a cool, dark place. It should be ready for drinking after 6 months.

Preparation: 30 minutes

Cooking: 15 minutes

Makes about I gallon (4.5 liters)

### INGREDIENTS

14 oranges (zest of 7 and juice of all)

4 quarts (4.5 liters) water

6½ cups (1.5kg) superfine (caster) sugar

I teaspoon wine yeast

I teaspoon yeast nutrient

I teaspoon pectic enzyme

# Mead (honey wine)

Preparation: 30 minutes

Cooking: 30 minutes

Makes about 1 gallon (4.5 liters)

INGREDIENTS
·····················

1¼ cups (500g) honey

4 quarts (4.5 liters) water

1 orange, sliced

1 teaspoon wine yeast

1 teaspoon yeast nutrient

1 stick cinnamon

2 cloves

pinch of ground nutmeg

pinch of ground allspice

pinch of powdered ginger

30 raisins

Probably the most ancient of alcoholic drinks—known to have been made in prehistoric times—mead is evocative of medieval banquets. It's a delightful drink, though making it requires patience, as it will take a long time to finish and then to mature. Try using different regional types of honey or floral honeys, such as orange blossom or lavender honey. Although mead is excellent served at room temperature, it can also be gently warmed to make a soothing treat on a winter's evening.

1. Put the honey and water into a large pan and bring to a gentle boil. Skim off any scum that emerges and then allow to cool.

2. Pour this mixture into a sterilized fermenting bucket (see page 12). Add the remaining ingredients and cover the bucket with its lid. Leave for 3–4 days.

3. Pour the contents, including the orange and solid spices, into a sterilized demijohn and fit an air lock (see page 14). Leave to ferment; this will take a lot longer than for other wines, perhaps up to 3 months.

4. When fermentation has ceased (the orange bits will have sunk to the bottom and there are no more bubbles), siphon off (see page 15) into sterilized bottles. Store in a cool, dark place. It should be ready for drinking after 6 months, but, ideally, leave for a year before opening. Your willpower will be rewarded.

# Chapter 2

# Syrups & Cordials

# Elderflower syrup

One of the earliest harvests you can employ in making syrups, elderflower evokes the promise of a long, lazy summer about to begin. This classic syrup is usually diluted with still or sparkling water, but for a more glamorous drink, add a drop to some chilled white wine.

Preparation: 20 minutes
Cooking: 15 minutes
Makes about 5 cups (1.2 liters)

### INGREDIENTS

20 heads of elderflower
(see page 11)

2 unwaxed lemons

10 cups (1.8kg) superfine (caster) sugar

5 cups (1.2 liters) water

3/8 cup (75g) citric acid

1. Shake the elderflower heads to remove any lingering insects, remove the stems, and place in a large mixing bowl. Peel the zest from the lemons, then slice them. Add the zest and lemon slices to the bowl.

2. Put the sugar and water into a pan and bring to a boil, stirring until all the sugar has dissolved.

3. Pour the sugar syrup over the elderflower heads and lemon, add the citric acid, and give the contents a good stir.

4. Cover the mixture with a clean dish towel and let steep for 24 hours.

5. Strain the mixture through a sieve lined with fine muslin or cheesecloth (see page 12).

6. Pour the syrup into sterilized bottles (see page 12) and store in a cool, dark place. Use within 3 months. Alternatively, freeze in small plastic containers (see page 13).

# Blueberry & elderflower syrup

Elderflower has a wonderful perfume, which beautifully complements the great flavor of blueberries. To take full advantage of its fleeting season, this recipe makes a large batch of syrup. A lovely way to enjoy this syrup is to pour a little in a blender, add some vanilla ice cream and some milk, and blitz briefly to combine. Garnish with a few blueberries and enjoy a scrumptious blueberry milkshake.

I. Remove the stems of the elderflowers as close to the heads as possible, then shake the flowers to remove any persistent insects. Place the flowers in a large mixing bowl. Cut the lemons into quarters.

2. Put the blueberries, sugar, lemon, citric acid, and water in a large pan. Bring to a boil then reduce the heat and let the mixture simmer for 15–20 minutes, squashing the berries with a potato masher or the back of a spoon.

3. Once all the berries are reduced to a pulp, pour the mixture into the bowl containing the elderflowers, making sure they are completely covered (use the back of a wooden spoon to push them in, if necessary). Cover the bowl with a clean dish towel and let steep overnight.

4. Strain the mixture through a fine sieve; if you want a really clear syrup, strain it again through a jelly bag (see page 12).

5. Pour the syrup into sterilized bottles (see page 12); use within 3 months. Alternatively, freeze in smaller containers (see page 13).

Preparation: 30 minutes

Cooking: 30 minutes

Makes about 10 cups (2.5 liters)

### INGREDIENTS

20 large heads of elderflower (preferably picked in the late afternoon, see page 11)

2 unwaxed lemons

3 cups (400g) blueberries (fresh or frozen)

2½ cups (550g) superfine (caster) sugar

I teaspoon citric acid

5 cups (1.2 liters) water

# Pear, raspberry, & elderflower syrup

Preparation: 10 minutes
Cooking: 25 minutes
Makes about 3⅓ cups (800ml)

## INGREDIENTS

1¼ pounds (600g) pears

20 heads of elderflower
(see page 11)

⅞ cup (200g) superfine (caster)
sugar

2 lemons, juice only

1 lime, zest only

¾ teaspoon citric acid

3 cups (750ml) water

1¾ cups (200g) raspberries

This recipe, featuring the delicate perfume of elderflowers, is one of my all-time favorites. You'll need to make it when elder is in bloom, so will probably have to use out-of-season pears and raspberries from the supermarket. Frozen raspberries are fine, but make sure that the pears are really ripe before using them. For a special treat, dilute this syrup with a little fermented pear juice, or perry, and lemon soda pop. Or mix it into crème anglaise (custard) to pour over a lovely pear crisp (crumble).

1. Chop the pears into little chunks (no need to peel or core). Shake the elderflower heads really well to ensure that any insects are removed, then place them in a bowl and set aside.

2. Put the sugar, lemon juice, lime zest, citric acid, and water in a pan and bring to a boil, stirring until all the sugar is dissolved. Reduce the heat, add the pears and raspberries, and simmer for 15 minutes. Remove from the heat and allow to cool for 20 minutes.

3. Pour the pear and raspberry mixture over the elderflowers. Cover with a clean dish towel and leave overnight to steep.

4. Strain the mixture through a fine sieve (see page 12); repeat if necessary to make sure all the elderflowers are removed.

5. Pour the syrup into sterilized bottles (see page 12) and store in a cool, dark place and use within 3 months.

# Lemon & lavender syrup

Preparation: 20 minutes

Cooking: 20 minutes

Makes about 6 cups (1.4 liters)

INGREDIENTS
.....................

10–12 heads of lavender

3 unwaxed lemons, juice and zest

1¼ cups (300g) superfine (caster) sugar

6 cups (1.4 liters) water

1½ teaspoons citric acid

I've always loved growing lavender in my garden; the heady scent when one brushes past it is intoxicating. I love the scent indoors, too. But once I started using it in cooking I was amazed by its versatility. Besides being useful for sweetening stewed fruit and other desserts, it complements many meat dishes, too; try it in a simple lamb casserole, for example. Be sure to use the common lavender, *Lavandula angustifolia*, rather than the more unusual species.

1. Rinse the lavender heads under cold running waterand set aside.

2. Put the lemon juice in a large pan and add the sugar, water, and citric acid. Bring to a boil. Add the lavender and allow to simmer for another 10 minutes. Remove from the heat and let cool for 1 hour.

3. Strain the syrup through a piece of muslin (see page 12).

4. Pour the syrup into sterilized bottles (see page 12) and store in a cool, dark place. Use within 3 months.

## Now try this

Embellish a drink made from this syrup and sparkling water with a slice of lemon and some ice cubes in which you have frozen some lavender heads. Or mix the cordial with some confectioners' (icing) sugar to make a simple icing for a cake.

# Lemon & thyme syrup

Preparation: 10 minutes
Cooking: 20 minutes
Makes about 6 cups (1.4 liters)

### INGREDIENTS

bunch of fresh thyme, or
4 teaspoons dried thyme

4½ cups (1 liter) lemon juice (about
16 lemons, preferably unwaxed)

zest from 4 of the lemons

2¼ cups (500g) superfine (caster)
sugar

2 cups (500ml) water

1 teaspoon citric acid

Despite its unconventional ingredient—an herb normally
associated with savory dishes—this syrup has won over many
a skeptic. Try it yourself; you may be surprised how much you
like it. For a piquant dessert, try adding some of this syrup to
the filling for lemon meringue tartlets.

1. Rinse the thyme, if using fresh (see page 11).

2. Put the lemon juice and zest in a large pan, along with the sugar,
thyme, water, and citric acid, and bring to a boil. Reduce heat and
simmer for 20 minutes. Remove from the heat, cover with a saucepan
lid or dish towel, and let cool for 2 hours.

3. Strain through a piece of muslin (see page 12).

4. Pour the syrup into sterilized bottles (see page 12). Store in
a cool, dark place. Use within 3 months.

# Honey & lemon syrup

Preparation: 10 minutes
Cooking: 20 minutes
Makes about 4 cups (1 liter)

### INGREDIENTS

1¹/₂ cups (500g) clear honey
1 large lemon, juice only
4 cups (1 liter) water
4 teaspoons tartaric acid

Note: you will need a microwave
to make this syrup.

We all know how soothing honey and lemon are when we have a cold, but they also make a surprisingly pleasant base for a cool drink. The taste will vary according to the kind of honey you select. Ordinary store-bought honey is fine, but you might like to try experimenting with lavender or lime honey, or source some honey from a local beekeeper. This syrup mixes well with vodka.

1. Heat the honey in the microwave at the 450w setting (remember to remove the lid first), for 1 minute only; the honey should not be any hotter than 158°F (70°C), as this would impair the flavor.

2. Pour the honey into a 1-quart (1-liter) pitcher (jug); add the lemon juice.

3. Boil the water, then allow it to cool until it is lukewarm. Add it, along with the tartaric acid, to the pitcher, filling it up to about 1 inch (3cm) from the top and stir well to blend thoroughly. If necessary, put the pitcher into the microwave for 1 minute to make sure the honey is dissolved.

4. Pour the contents into sterilized bottles (see page 12) and store in a cool, dark place. Use within 3 months. I do not recommend freezing this syrup, as it would cause the honey to crystallize and could impair the flavor.

#### Now try this

Use this to jazz up some plain sponge cake—or lemon drizzle cake: pierce lots of holes in the top of the cake, then pour the syrup evenly into the holes.

# Ginger syrup

Preparation: 10 minutes

Cooking: 20 minutes

Makes about 2½ cups (600ml)

INGREDIENTS

3 ounces (85g) gingerroot, or more
to taste

1¼ cups (300g) superfine (caster)
sugar

1¾ cups (400ml) water

1¾ cups (400ml) lemon juice
(about 9 or 10 lemons)

¾ teaspoon citric acid

Gingerroot has long been used in folk medicine and is a great soother of the stomach. But unlike many medicinal herbs and spices, ginger is delicious and makes a fantastic syrup—great for long car journeys. I like this one very fiery and use a bit more ginger than I've specified here. With its lemon content this syrup pairs beautifully with lemon soda (lemonade) and a slice of lemon. You might also pour a little over lemon sorbet and top with some crystallized ginger.

1. Coarsely mash the gingerroot using a mortar and pestle.

2. Put the ginger in a pan along with the sugar and water and bring to a boil. Reduce the heat and allow to simmer for 15 minutes.

3. Add the lemon juice and citric acid and bring the mixture back to a boil. Allow to cool for 1 hour.

4. Strain the mixture through a piece of fine muslin or cheesecloth (see page 12).

5. Pour the syrup into sterilized bottles and store in a cool, dark place; use within 3 months.

# Gooseberry & lemon balm syrup

If gooseberries are not readily available from local supermarkets, why not grow your own? (Check with a garden center to find a good cultivar for your area.) This underestimated fruit has many uses—in desserts and sauces for meat and fish. It also has health benefits, being packed with fiber and vitamins A and C.

Preparation: 10 minutes
Cooking: 25 minutes
Makes about 5 cups (1.2 liters)

### INGREDIENTS

1³/₄ cups (400g) gooseberries

8 sprigs fresh lemon balm (preferably young leaves)

1¹/₄ cups (280g) superfine (caster) sugar

1 unwaxed lemon, juice and zest

1 teaspoon citric acid

4 cups (1 liter) water

1. Wash the gooseberries; there is no need to trim (top and tail) them. Shake the lemon balm to remove any insects; lay the sprigs on a flat surface and crush with a rolling pin; set aside.

2. Put the gooseberries in a pan along with the sugar, lemon juice and zest, citric acid, and water. Bring to a boil, then reduce the heat and leave the mixture to simmer for 10 minutes, or until the gooseberries are soft. Mash with the back of a spoon. Remove from the heat and let cool for about 45 minutes.

3. Strain the mixture through a piece of fine muslin or cheesecloth (see page 12), pushing on the pulp to extract every last bit of flavor.

4. Pour the syrup into sterilized bottles (see page 12) and store in a cool, dark place. Use within 3 months. Alternatively, it can be frozen (see page 13).

## Now try this

Try using some of this cordial as a marinade for mackerel to be cooked on the barbecue. Then you could also add some to white wine to drink with the fish.

# Gooseberry & elderflower syrup

If you're lucky enough to live in a part of the country where fresh gooseberries are readily available, make the most of them by making this light, refreshing syrup. The syrup works especially well diluted with sparkling white wine. You could also add some to a salad of mixed cantaloupe and honeydew melon (use a melon baller for a pretty effect) and prosciutto.

I. Rinse the gooseberries under cold water. There is no need to trim (top and tail) them. Wash the elderflowers (see page II) and put them in a large mixing bowl.

2. Put the gooseberries, sugar, lemon juice and zest, and water in a large pan and bring to a boil. Reduce the heat and simmer for 15 minutes. Make sure that all the gooseberries have softened to a pulp, mashing them with the back of the spoon, if necessary. Remove from the heat and let cool for 1 hour.

3. Pour the gooseberry mixture over the elderflowers. Cover with a clean dish towel and let steep overnight.

4. Strain the mixture through a sieve lined with fine muslin or cheesecloth (see page 12).

5. Pour the syrup into sterilized bottles (see page 12) and store in a cool, dark place. Use within 3 months.

Preparation: 10 minutes
Cooking: 20 minutes
Makes about 5 cups (1.2 liters)

### INGREDIENTS

1³/₄ cups (400g) gooseberries

5 or 6 large heads of elderflower
(see page II)

1¹/₄ cups (280g) superfine (caster)
sugar

I unwaxed lemon, juice and zest

4 cups (I liter) water

I teaspoon citric acid

# Blackberry & lime syrup

Blackberries can be found in abundance from late summer into fall. Children especially love to pick blackberries, although most go into the mouth even before they can get to the kitchen. Try using this syrup on lime sorbet or chocolate ice cream. Alternatively, blend it with cider vinegar to make a dressing for a special salad; it goes particularly well with duck.

Preparation: 10 minutes

Cooking: 30 minutes

Makes about 6½ cups (1.5 liters)

### INGREDIENTS

12 cups (1.5kg) blackberries

1 lime

7 cups (1.6 liters) water

1¾ cups (400g) superfine (caster) sugar

1½ teaspoons citric acid

1. Pick over the blackberries, discarding any rotten ones. Rinse them under cold running water, being careful not to break their skins, as you need to retain as much juice as possible. Grate about 1 teaspoon of zest from the lime, then squeeze the lime to extract the juice.

2. Place the berries in a pan and cover them with the water. Bring them to a boil and allow to simmer until they burst, using a potato masher to facilitate this if necessary.

3. Strain the berry juice through a metal sieve into a clean saucepan (see page 12).

4. Add the sugar, lime juice and zest, and citric acid to the berry juice. Bring to a boil and stir until the sugar has dissolved. Let the syrup cool for at least 1 hour.

5. Pour the syrup into sterilized bottles (see page 12) and store in a cool, dark place, where it will keep for up to 3 months. Alternatively, place it in plastic containers (see page 13) and freeze it.

# Strawberry & black pepper syrup

Preparation: 15 minutes

Cooking: 45 minutes

Makes about 5 cups (1.2 liters)

### INGREDIENTS

$4^{1}/_{2}$ cups (500g) strawberries (5 cups if large)

4 cups (900g) superfine (caster) sugar

$^{1}/_{2}$ teaspoon freshly ground black pepper

1 unwaxed lemon

2 cups (500ml) water

$1^{1}/_{2}$ teaspoons citric acid

More than any other fruit, strawberries seem to conjure up the essence of summer. Black pepper might seem an unusual ingredient to add to strawberries, but it brings out the sweetness of the berries, intensifying their flavor.

1. Mash the strawberries and sugar together in a bowl, using a potato masher. Sprinkle the black pepper over the mixture and gently stir in.

2. Cut the lemon into wedges and put them in a saucepan with the water. Bring to a boil and then simmer for 15 minutes.

3. Add the strawberry mixture and the citric acid to the lemon and water. Stir in and bring to a gentle simmer; let simmer for another 25 minutes. Remove from the heat. Cover with a clean dish towel and allow to cool for at least 2 hours.

4. Strain the cooled syrup through a fine sieve, pressing gently on the pulp in the sieve to squeeze out the last few drops of liquid (see page 12).

5. Pour the syrup into sterilized bottles (see page 12) and store in a cool, dark place. To serve, dilute to taste. Use within 3 months of making.

### Now try this

This cordial is delicious on meringues or simply drizzled on plain yogurt.

# Strawberry & mint syrup

Bought strawberries, in season, are fine; but if possible, grow your own. There is a special excitement to be had from lifting a leaf in a strawberry patch and finding a plump, warm fruit waiting to be picked. In this syrup the mellow flavor of strawberries is given extra zing with fresh mint. Try blending some of this syrup into some plain yogurt. Serve with a sprig of mint and some pistachio cookies on the side.

Preparation: 10 minutes
Cooking: 25 minutes
Makes about 3 cups (700ml)

INGREDIENTS

5 sprigs fresh mint

5/8 rounded cup (150g) superfine (caster) sugar

1/2 unwaxed lemon

3 cups (700ml) water

4 1/2 cups (500g) strawberries (5 cups if large)

1/2 teaspoon citric acid

I. Rinse the mint under cold running water and put it in a pan with the sugar, half lemon, and water. Bring to a boil and stir until all the sugar has dissolved.

2. Reduce the heat and add the strawberries and citric acid. Simmer until all the strawberries are soft. Cover with a clean dish towel and let cool and steep overnight.

3. Strain the syrup through a sieve (see page 12).

4. Pour into sterilized bottles (see page 12) and store in a cool, dark place; use within 3 months. Alternatively, freeze in small portions (see page 13).

# Strawberry & lavender syrup

The versatility of lavender is quite amazing. It is used in perfume, to scent linens, as a room fragrance, and even in baking. Here, it gives a lovely aromatic note to a strawberry syrup. This recipe will give you a renewed appreciation of this little flower.

I. Put the lemon juice and zest, sugar, and water in a pan; boil until the sugar has dissolved.

2. Add the strawberries, lavender, and citric acid and simmer for 20 minutes. Use a potato masher to crush the strawberries as they cook. Remove from the heat and allow the mixture to cool for 30 minutes.

3. Strain the mixture through a sieve, gently pushing on the pulp to squeeze out the last few drops of juice (see page 12).

4. Pour the syrup into sterilized bottles (see page 12), and store in a cool, dark place. Use within 3 months.

Preparation: 15 minutes
Cooking: 35 minutes
Makes about 3 cups (700ml)

### INGREDIENTS

1/2 unwaxed lemon, juice and zest

5/8 cup, rounded (150g) superfine (caster) sugar

2 cups (500ml) water

4 1/2 cups (500g) hulled strawberries (5 cups if large)

20 heads of lavender (see page 11)

1/2 teaspoon citric acid

## Now try this

Try diluting the syrup with white wine and soda water. Or add a little to a cup of hot chocolate and top with whipped cream. Add a few lavender flowers as a garnish.

# Rhubarb syrup

One of the earliest arrivals in the kitchen garden, rhubarb is most often stewed or used in baking. However, it makes a delicious syrup, with a beautiful pink hue. Try mixing this syrup with vodka, adding plenty of ice, for a summer cocktail party.

I. Remove the leaves and trim the bottom edges of the rhubarb; chop roughly. Cut the lemon into quarters. Slit the vanilla bean lengthwise and scrape out the seeds for use in the syrup.

2. Put the rhubarb, lemon, sugar, cloves, vanilla seeds, and water into a pan. Bring to a boil, being careful not to burn the rhubarb.

3. Once the sugar has completely dissolved, add the citric acid and turn the heat down to a gentle simmer. Continue simmering for 20 minutes or until all of the rhubarb is soft. Remove from the heat and allow to cool for 2 hours.

4. Strain the mixture through a sieve (see page 12). If you like your syrup clear, strain again through a piece of fine muslin or cheesecloth.

5. Pour the syrup into sterilized bottles (see page 12) and store in a cool, dark place. It will last there for up to 3 months. Alternatively, you can freeze some of the syrup to make it last longer (see page 13).

Preparation: 10 minutes
Cooking: 45 minutes
Makes about 3½ cups (900ml)

### INGREDIENTS

I pound (450g) rhubarb

I unwaxed lemon

I vanilla bean

2 cups, rounded (480g) superfine (caster) sugar

2 cloves

3¾ cups (900ml) water

I teaspoon citric acid

## Now try this

For a self-indulgent dessert, add
it to crushed meringues and top
with a dollop of crème fraîche
or whipped cream.

# Rhubarb, lemon, & rosemary syrup

Preparation: 15 minutes
Cooking: 20 minutes
Makes about 5 cups (1.2 liters)

### INGREDIENTS

2 large sprigs fresh rosemary
1 pound (450g) rhubarb
2 cups, rounded (450g) superfine
(caster) sugar
2 unwaxed lemons, juice and zest
4 cups (1 liter) water
1 teaspoon citric acid

I love to baffle guests with this syrup. Most can quickly recognize the rhubarb and lemon flavors; but the astonished looks when I reveal the mystery ingredient, rosemary, are quite amusing. You, too, may be amazed at how successful this combination is. Rosemary signifies love, friendship, and trust, so make this for a special person. For a delicious teatime treat, keep the pulp (removing the rosemary stalks), and add to a sponge cake recipe.

1. Rinse the rosemary, and chop the rhubarb into chunks.

2. Put these ingredients in a large pan, along with the sugar, lemon juice and zest, water, and citric acid, and bring to a boil. Remove from the heat and allow to cool for 2 hours.

3. Strain through a sieve lined with muslin (see page 12); give the remaining pulp a good squeeze to extract all of the juice.

4. Pour into sterilized bottles (see page 12). Store in a cool, dark place. Use within 3 months.

# Passion fruit syrup

Although passion fruit is not native to northern climes, you can find it in larger supermarkets year-round. The unassuming exterior of the fruit hides a scrumptious center with an equally mouthwatering aroma, and this surprisingly easy-to-make syrup has an outstanding finish. Try adding some of this syrup to sparkling white wine for a refreshing grown-up picnic treat. Or pour a little over chocolate ice cream.

1. Cut the passion fruits in half and scrape the pulp into a bowl.

2. Put the sugar, lemon juice, and water into a pan. Bring to a boil, stirring until all the sugar has dissolved.

3. Turn down the heat and add the passion fruit pulp. Stir until well mixed, keeping at a gentle simmer for another 20 minutes.

4. Remove from the heat, cover with a clean dish towel, and let steep overnight.

5. Strain through a fine sieve, pushing gently on the pulp to squeeze out all the juice (see page 12).

6. Pour into sterilized bottles (see page 12) and store in a cool, dark place. Once opened, use within 4 weeks. Alternatively, freeze in small batches for later use (see page 13).

Preparation: 20 minutes
Cooking: 25 minutes
Makes about 3 cups (700ml)

INGREDIENTS

16 passion fruits

1 cup (225g) superfine (caster) sugar

1 cup (240ml) fresh lemon juice

1½ cups (360ml) water

# Mango & ginger syrup

Preparation: 10 minutes

Cooking: 25 minutes

Makes about 6 cups (1.4 liters)

### INGREDIENTS

1 large, very ripe mango—approx.
1¼ pound (570g)

2-inch (5-cm) piece gingerroot

1 vanilla bean

1⅝ cups (375g) superfine (caster)
sugar

1 unwaxed lemon

¾ teaspoon citric acid

2 cups (500ml) water

This recipe has a tropical note, conjuring up images of white, sandy beaches and an azure sea. It makes a perfect drink for a lazy afternoon in a hammock. Mix the syrup with coconut milk and freeze to make ice pops (ice lollies).

1. Peel the mango and cut the flesh away from the pit. Peel the ginger and crush the flesh with a rolling pin, or use a mortar and pestle. Slice the vanilla bean in half lengthwise and scrape out the seeds; reserve. Cut the lemon into quarters.

2. Put the mango, ginger, vanilla seeds, lemon, sugar, citric acid, and water in a pan. Bring to a boil, stirring until all the sugar is dissolved. Reduce the heat and simmer for another 20 minutes, stirring constantly. Remove from the heat and allow to cool for 30 minutes.

3. Strain the mixture through a fine sieve (see page 12).

4. Pour the syrup into sterilized bottles (see page 12), then store in a cool, dark place. Use within 1 month.

## Now try this

Drizzle it over a salad of lettuce, fresh mango, and halloumi cheese. It will give a sweet and mildly spicy kick to a summer lunch.

# Black currant syrup

Preparation: 30 minutes

Cooking: 20 minutes

Makes about 6½ cups (1.5 liters)

### INGREDIENTS

6 cups (900g) black currants

2 cups, rounded (500g) superfine
(caster) sugar

3 cups (700ml) water

1 unwaxed lemon, juice and zest

1 teaspoon citric acid

Although very popular in Britain, black currants are not widely known in the United States (though the prohibitions against growing them, for ecological reasons, have now generally been lifted). If you can grow black currants in your state, do plant one of these shrubs. The berries have a rich, complex flavor—sweet, savory, and tart—and they have many health benefits, being especially high in vitamin C.

I. Remove all the stalks from the berries and gently wash the fruit.

2. Put the berries in a large pan, along with the sugar and water, and heat slowly until all the sugar has dissolved. Then turn up the heat and bring the mixture to a gentle simmer; let it simmer for 5 minutes.

3. Add the lemon juice and zest and the citric acid and bring the mixture back to a simmer for another 5 minutes. Remove from the heat and let cool for 10 minutes.

4. Strain through a sieve lined with fine muslin or cheesecloth, pushing the pulp with the back of a spoon to get the last of the juice, while keeping out the pulp as much as possible (see page 12).

5. Pour the syrup into sterilized bottles (see page 12) and store in a cool, dark place. Use within 3 months. Alternatively store in plastic bottles in the freezer.

### Now try this

Try using this syrup in a
marinade for pork or drizzle a
little over some ginger ice cream.

# Summer syrup

It's a wonderful thing, on a hot summer's day, to stand among rows of raspberries, with just the humming of a passing bee for company, eating as many raspberries as you put into your basket. Or blackberries, or cherries… Freeze some of this cordial in an ice-cube tray. Then put a few ice cubes in a highball glass and fill it up with lemon soda (fizzy lemonade); the ice cubes will melt, creating a delightful color contrast.

I. Rinse the fruit carefully under running water. Remove the stalks from the cherries; there is no need to remove the pits, which will be strained out. Cut the lemons into quarters.

2. Put the fruit in a large pan with the sugar, fennel seed, cardamom pods, and water. Bring the mixture to a boil, stirring to make sure the sugar has dissolved. Turn down the heat, add the citric acid, and allow to simmer for another 20 minutes. Remove from the heat, cover with a clean dish towel, and allow to cool for at least 2 hours.

3. Strain through a fine sieve, pressing firmly on the pulp to make sure all the juice is squeezed out. To clarify further, strain again through a jelly bag or a piece of fine muslin or cheesecloth (see page 12).

4. Pour into sterilized bottles (see page 12); store in a cool, dark place. Use within 3 months. Alternatively, freeze in an ice-cube tray (see page 13).

Preparation: 30–40 minutes
Cooking: 25 minutes
Makes about 7½ cups (1.8 liters)

### INGREDIENTS

3 cups (400g) cherries

2½ cups, rounded (300g) raspberries

2½ cups, rounded (300g) strawberries

2½ cups (300g) blackberries

2 cups (300g) red currants (or mixed black and red currants)

2 unwaxed lemons

1¾ cups (400g) superfine (caster) sugar

½ teaspoon fennel seeds

2 cardamom pods

5 cups (1.2 liters) water

1½ teaspoons citric acid

# Autumn harvest syrup

Preparation: 40 minutes
Cooking: 30 minutes
Makes about 10 cups (2.4 liters)

## INGREDIENTS

1 pound 2 ounces (500g) apples
(6 small)

14 ounces (400g) plums
(4 medium size)

3 cups (350g) blackberries

1 cup (150g) black currants or red
currants

1 unwaxed lemon

2¼ cups (500g) superfine (caster)
sugar

6½ cups (1.5 liters) water

1 stick cinnamon

6 allspice berries

1 star anise

2 teaspoons citric acid

Fall is the most plentiful time of the year when it comes to free fruit; almost everywhere you look there will be a glut of fruit to make use of. Perhaps you have an apple, pear, or plum tree that needs picking—or a neighbor has one. Or you may have a bramble patch full of delicious blackberries at the end of your garden that has not been cleared during the summer. All of these and more can be found close by and will give you a valuable harvest, well worth the effort.

1. Core and peel the apples. Wash and halve the plums, removing the pits. Rinse the blackberries and the currants in water. Cut the lemon into quarters.

2. Put the sugar, lemon, and spices in a pan, along with the water. Bring to a boil and stir until all of the sugar has dissolved. Reduce the heat. Add the apples, plums, blackberries, currants, and citric acid and simmer for another 20 minutes, or until all the fruit has been reduced to a pulp.

3. Remove from the heat, cover with a clean dish towel, and allow to cool for 2 hours.

4. Strain the mixture through a fine sieve, taking care to squeeze as much juice out of the pulp as possible (see page 12). Then strain again, this time through a jelly bag or piece of fine muslin or cheesecloth.

5. Pour the syrup into sterilized bottles (see page 12) and store it in a cool, dark place. It will usually last into the cold winter months. For added longevity it could be frozen (see page 13).

## Now try this

This syrup can be diluted with hot water to make a warming winter drink. Or you can add gelatin to the diluted syrup to make a delicious jellied dessert.

# Mulberry & cardamom syrup

Preparation: 5 minutes
Cooking: 20 minutes
Makes about 3¹/₂ cups (800ml)

INGREDIENTS

5 cups (600g) mulberries
4 cardmom pods
⁷/₈ cup (200g) superfine (caster) sugar
2 cups (500ml) water
I unwaxed lemon
¹/₂ teaspoon citric acid

Fresh mulberries can be hard to find, but if you're fortunate enough to have a bush growing in your garden or know of someone who has, do make some of this exotic syrup. Warning: picking mulberries is a really messy job, so go prepared and do not wear white! I love to make meringues flavored with cardamom seed and serve them with whipped cream, a few mulberries, a drizzle of the syrup, and, to finish, a few chopped pistachios on top.

I. Cut the lemon into quarters.

2. Put the mulberries, cardamom pods, sugar, lemon pieces, and water in a pan. Bring to a boil, stirring continuously until the sugar has dissolved. Reduce the heat and let simmer for another I5 minutes. Mash any whole mulberries with the back of the spoon. Do the same with the cardamom pods as they become soft.

3. Once the mulberries have been reduced to a pulp, remove the pan from the heat and cover with a saucepan lid or dish towel. Let cool for about 2 hours.

4. Strain the mixture through a fine sieve and then through a jelly bag or piece of fine muslin or cheesecloth (see page I2).

5. Pour the syrup into sterilized bottles (see page I2) and store in a cool, dark place. Use within 3 months.

# Orange, echinacea, & lemongrass syrup

We all know that echinacea is reputed to be effective against coughs and colds. In addition, it has a lovely earthy taste that offsets the sharpness of the oranges in this syrup. Pour some of this syrup sparingly over half a grapefruit for a refreshing taste treat.

I. Rinse the lemongrass in water and crush it with a rolling pin.

2. Put it in a large pan along with the orange juice and zest, sugar, citric acid, and water. Bring to a boil, stirring until all the sugar has dissolved. Reduce the heat and add the echinacea. Simmer, stirring, for another 5 minutes. Remove from the heat and allow to cool for I hour.

3. Strain the mixture through a fine sieve, pushing gently with the spoon to extract all of the juice, then strain again through a jelly bag or a piece of fine muslin or cheesecloth (see page 12).

4. Pour the syrup into sterilized bottles (see page 12) and store in a cool, dark place. Use within 3 months.

Preparation: 30 minutes
Cooking: 20 minutes
Makes about 7¹/₂ cups (1.8 liters)

### INGREDIENTS

I stem lemongrass

16 oranges: zest of 2, juice of all

2¹/₄ cups (500g) superfine (caster) sugar

I¹/₂ teaspoons citric acid

2 cups (450ml) water

¹/₂ cup (40g) shredded echinacea root

# Raspberry & angelica syrup

If you haven't got fresh raspberries, you can use frozen ones for this syrup, as raspberries have the ability to hold on to their luscious flavor even after they have been in a freezer. I really enjoy the slight hint of celery that the angelica gives to this syrup—a subtle, earthy taste that, however, doesn't detract from the tang of the raspberries. A little of this syrup makes a good addition to a shot of vodka.

Preparation: 10 minutes
Cooking: 20 minutes
Makes about 2¹/₂ cups (600ml)

INGREDIENTS

3¹/₂ cups (400g) raspberries

a small bunch of angelica leaves
(about 4–5)

1¹/₄ cups, rounded (300g) superfine
(caster) sugar

1 unwaxed lemon, juice and zest

1³/₄ cups (400ml) water

³/₄ teaspoon citric acid

1. Rinse the angelica leaves under running water. Put them in a pan along with the raspberries, sugar, lemon juice and zest, water, and citric acid. Bring to a boil, stirring constantly until all the sugar has dissolved. Reduce the heat and simmer for another 15 minutes, stirring occasionally. Mash any whole raspberries with the back of the spoon.

2. Remove from the heat, cover with a saucepan lid or dish towel, and let cool for about 2 hours.

3. Strain the syrup through a fine sieve (see page 12) and then through a jelly bag or a piece of fine muslin or cheesecloth.

4. Pour the syrup into sterilized bottles (see page 12) and store it in a cool, dry place; use within 3 months.

Now try this
For a glamorous dessert, add a few raspberries to the syrup and make into a coulis. Pour it onto individual portions of cheesecake and garnish with a few angelica leaves.

# Raspberry & lovage syrup

I love the fragrantly sweet, yet slightly tart flavor of raspberries; there never seems to be enough of them. If you can bear to put some aside for this syrup, you won't be disappointed. Show off its glorious color in a beautiful glass bottle. For a delectable dessert, combine some crushed meringues and sliced peaches and top them with whipped cream mixed with this syrup.

I. Rinse the lovage leaves under running water. Put the raspberries, lovage, sugar, lemon juice and zest, and water in a pan. Bring to a boil, stirring continuously until all the sugar has dissolved. Reduce the heat, add the citric acid, and let simmer for another 15 minutes, stirring occasionally and mashing any whole raspberries with the back of the spoon.

2. When the raspberries have been reduced to a pulp, remove from the heat and cover with a saucepan lid or dish towel. Allow to cool for about 2 hours.

3. Strain the mixture through a fine sieve and then through a jelly bag or piece of fine muslin or cheesecloth (see page 12).

4. Pour the syrup into sterilized bottles (see page 12). Store in a cool, dark place; use within 3 months.

Preparation: 10 minutes
Cooking: 20 minutes
Makes about 2¹/₂ cups (600ml)

INGREDIENTS

3¹/₂ cups (400g) raspberries

a handful of fresh lovage leaves
(about 10–15)

1¹/₃ cups (300g) superfine (caster)
sugar

1 lemon, juice and zest

1³/₄ cups (400ml) water

³/₄ teaspoon citric acid

# Raspberry & rose syrup

Preparation: 10 minutes
Cooking: 20 minutes
Makes about 4 cups (1 liter)

### INGREDIENTS

6 cups (700g) raspberries

1⅓ cups (300g) superfine (caster) sugar

2 unwaxed lemons, zest and juice

1 teaspoon citric acid

2 cups (500ml) water

4 cups, rounded (50g) red rose petals

The aroma and flavor of the rose petals really shine through in this syrup, softening the tart edge of the strong-flavored fruit, without imposing an overtly floral taste on it. Dilute the syrup to taste with sparkling or soda water.

1. Put the raspberries, sugar, lemon juice and zest, citric acid, and water in a saucepan. Bring to a boil, then simmer for 15 minutes.

2. Remove from the heat and let cool for 30 minutes.

3. Put the rose petals in a large bowl and pour the syrup over them. Cover with a clean dish towel and let steep overnight.

4. Strain the syrup through a piece of fine muslin or cheesecloth (see page 12).

5. Pour the syrup into sterilized bottles (see page 12). It will keep in a cool, dark place for up to 3 months.

## Now try this

Mix the syrup with water and gelatin, following the instructions on the packet. When the mixture starts to set, add in a few extra rose petals so they are suspended in it. (A glass bowl will display the effect beautifully.) Serve with vanilla ice cream.

# Raspberry & orange syrup

Preparation: 15 minutes
Cooking: 20 minutes
Makes about 4 cups (1 liter)

### INGREDIENTS

6 cups (700g) raspberries
1 1/3 cups (300g) superfine (caster) sugar
2 cups (500ml) water
6 oranges, zest and juice
1 teaspoon citric acid

Combining these two strong-flavored fruits creates a real taste sensation. This is a good way to use up a surplus of raspberries to prevent them from going off. Children can enjoy using it to make their own ice pops and lollies. Dilute the juice to taste with sparkling water. Or add a drop or two to an orange liqueur, then fill up the glass with lemon soda (fizzy lemonade).

I. Put the raspberries, sugar, and water in a saucepan. Bring to the boil and cook until all the raspberries have been reduced to a pulp. Reduce the heat and add the orange juice and zest and citric acid. Bring back to a boil.

2. Allow the syrup to cool for around 30–45 minutes then strain it through a piece of fine muslin or cheesecloth (see page 12).

3. Pour the syrup into sterilized bottles (see page 12). It will keep for up to 3 months when stored in a cool, dark place.

# Fig, peach, & vanilla syrup

This combination creates a deliciously smooth flavor—the vanilla taking the sharp edge off the peaches and the figs lending their own subtle, mellow taste. Hide this one, as you won't want to share it! Try pouring a little of this syrup over peaches or figs baked in puff pastry, dusted with confectioners' (icing) sugar.

Preparation: 10 minutes

Cooking: 20 minutes

Makes about 3⅓ cups (800ml)

### INGREDIENTS

14 ounces (400g) figs (14–16)

¾ pound (340g) peaches (3 small)

½ vanilla bean

1 unwaxed lemon, juice and zest

⅓ cup (80g) superfine (caster) sugar

3½ cups (820ml) water

¾ teaspoon citric acid

1. Trim the stalks from the figs. Peel the peaches, remove the pits, and cut into quarters. Scrape the seeds from the vanilla bean half and reserve.

2. Put the lemon juice and zest, sugar, and water in a pan and bring to a boil, stirring until all the sugar has dissolved. Reduce the heat and add the figs, peaches, vanilla seeds, and citric acid. Simmer until the fruit is soft, about 15 minutes.

3. Remove from the heat and let cool for 30 minutes.

4. Strain the mixture through a fine sieve (see page 12).

5. Pour the syrup into sterilized bottles (see page 12) and store in a cool, dark place. Use within 3 months.

# Lemonades

# Classic lemonade

Preparation: 20 minutes

Cooking: 20 minutes

Makes about 5 cups (1.2 liters)

INGREDIENTS
........................

zest of 1 unwaxed lemon

1³/₄ cups (400g) superfine (caster)
sugar

2¹/₃ cups (550ml) water

2¹/₃ cups (550ml) lemon juice
(about 12 lemons)

Although a little time consuming initially, compared to the simplest form of fresh lemonade, this recipe for a lemon syrup will enable you to conjure up a pitcher of refreshing lemonade at short notice on a hot summer's day. And if your children normally swig lemon soda (fizzy lemonade), they may enjoy discovering this natural alternative. Dilute the lemonade to taste with still, sparkling, or soda water. You can also use it, diluted 1 part lemonade to 2 parts water, to make ice pops (ice lollies).

1. Put the lemon zest, sugar, and water in a pan. Bring to a boil. Simmer, stirring, until all the sugar has dissolved.

2. Add the lemon juice, including some of the flesh if you prefer the lemonade to have a little texture, and bring the mixture back to a boil, stirring constantly.

3. Remove from the heat and allow to cool for 1 hour.

4. Pour the liquid into sterilized bottles (see page 12). It will keep in a cool, dark place or in the fridge for up to 2 months.

# Rose lemonade

Preparation: 20 minutes

Cooking: 20 minutes

Makes about 5 cups (1.2 liters)

### INGREDIENTS

zest of I unwaxed lemon

1³/₄ cups (400g) superfine (caster)
sugar

2¹/₃ cups (550ml) water

2¹/₃ cups (550ml) lemon juice
(about 12 lemons)

4¹/₂ cups (50g) rose petals
(see Note)

Note:
If you are using fresh rose petals,
make sure they have not been
sprayed with any chemicals; if in
doubt, buy dried rose petals from
a good herbalist.

This lemonade has a lovely perfume, and if you like floral
drinks it will become a favorite.

1. Put the lemon zest, sugar, and water in a pan and bring to a
boil. Simmer, stirring, until all the sugar has dissolved.

2. Add the lemon juice, including some of the flesh if you prefer
the lemonade to have a little texture, and bring the mixture back to
a boil, stirring constantly.

3. Remove from the heat and allow to cool for 1 hour.

4. Put the rose petals in a large bowl. Pour the liquid over the petals,
cover the bowl with a clean dish cloth, and let steep overnight.

5. Strain the liquid through a fine sieve (see page 12) and pour
into sterilized bottles (see page 12). It will keep in a cool, dark place
or in the fridge for up to 2 months.

# Lavender lemonade

Preparation: 30 minutes

Cooking: 25 minutes

Makes about 5 cups (1.2 liters)

### INGREDIENTS

zest of I unwaxed lemon

1³/₄ cups (400g) superfine (caster)
sugar

2¹/₃ cups (550ml) water

2¹/₃ cups (550ml) lemon juice
(about 12 lemons)

15 heads of lavender (see page 11)

Although I enjoy the beauty and the lovely scent of lavender
in the garden, I'm always looking for new and interesting ways
to use it in my cooking. Garnish your diluted lemonade with
a couple of heads of lavender. Or freeze some of the flowers
into ice cubes—this looks stunning.

1. Put the lemon zest, sugar, and water in a pan and bring to
a boil. Simmer, stirring, until all the sugar has dissolved.

2. Add the lemon juice, including some of the flesh if you prefer
the lemonade to have a little texture, and bring the mixture back
to a boil, stirring constantly.

3. Remove from the heat and add the lavender heads. Allow to
cool for 1 hour.

4. Strain the mixture (see page 12), then pour it into sterilized
bottles (see page 12). It will keep in a cool, dark place or in the
fridge for up to 2 months.

# Lavender & ginger lemonade

This is a truly delightful mix of flavors that work really well together. Give it a try—this may become the favorite of the summer. But you can also enjoy it in the depths of winter, when we are craving the start of spring and the delights of summer. Simply place the lavender heads in a jar along with the sugar and leave the jar in a cool, dark place until needed. Ginger, of course, is available throughout the year. Dilute with water as usual; or, for grown-ups, add to a shot of vodka. Finish with plenty of ice and a sprinkling of lavender flowers.

Preparation: 20 minutes

Cooking: 20 minutes

Makes about 5 cups (1.2 liters)

### INGREDIENTS

2-inch (5-cm) piece of fresh gingerroot

1³/4 cups (400g) superfine (caster) sugar

zest of 1 unwaxed lemon

2¹/3 cups (550ml) water

2¹/3 cups (550ml) lemon juice (about 12 lemons)

15 heads of lavender (see page 11)

I. Peel the ginger and crush it with a rolling pin. Put it in a pan with the sugar, lemon zest, and water. Bring to a boil. Simmer, stirring, to make sure all the sugar has dissolved.

2. Add the lemon juice, including some of the flesh if you prefer the lemonade to have a little texture, and bring the mixture back to a boil, stirring constantly.

3. Remove from the heat and allow to cool for 1 hour.

4. Place the lavender in one or more sterilized bottles (see page 12). Remove the pieces of ginger from the pan and discard.

5. Pour the liquid into the bottle(s). It will keep in a cool, dark place or in the fridge for up to 2 months.

# Pink lemonade

Cranberries give this lemonade a lovely color as well as extra flavor and pizzazz. This is great for taking on a picnic or serving at a special summer afternoon party. So plan ahead: freeze some cranberries in December for use in summer. Dilute to taste with your choice of water. You might also make it into a granita: put the diluted lemonade into an ice cream maker until it is slushy.

Preparation: 20 minutes

Cooking: 20 minutes

Makes about 5 cups (1.2 liters)

### INGREDIENTS

2 cups (200g) cranberries

2¼ cups (500g) superfine (caster) sugar

zest of 1 unwaxed lemon

2⅓ cups (550ml) water

2⅓ cups (550ml) lemon juice (about 12 lemons)

1. Put the cranberries, sugar, lemon zest, and water in a pan. Bring to a boil. Simmer, stirring, until all the sugar has dissolved and all the cranberries have split. Give them some help with a potato masher, if necessary.

2. Add the lemon juice, including some of the flesh if you prefer the lemonade to have a little texture, and bring the mixture back to a boil, stirring constantly.

3. Remove from the heat and allow to cool for 1 hour.

4. Strain the liquid through a fine sieve (see page 12). Add the lemon flesh, if desired, at this point.

5. Pour the liquid into sterilized bottles. It will keep in a cool, dark place or in the fridge for up to 2 months.

# Geranium lemonade

This ingenious recipe always gets a surprised reaction from guests, as many people do not realize that scented geraniums can be used for culinary purposes. I like to keep a good selection in my sun room. Try some of the different varieties, such as "Orange Fizz" and "Concolor Lace."

Preparation: 20 minutes
Cooking: 20 minutes
Makes about 5 cups (1.2 liters)

### INGREDIENTS

zest of 1 unwaxed lemon

2$^{1}/_{2}$ cups (550g) superfine (caster) sugar

2$^{1}/_{3}$ cups (550ml) water

2$^{1}/_{3}$ cups (550ml) lemon juice (about 12 lemons)

10 scented geranium leaves in good condition

1. Put the lemon zest, sugar, and water in a pan and bring to a boil. Simmer, stirring, until all the sugar has dissolved.

2. Add the lemon juice, including some of the flesh if you prefer the lemonade to have a little texture, and bring the mixture back to a boil, stirring constantly.

3. Remove from the heat and allow to cool for 1 hour.

4. Place the geranium leaves in a bowl. Pour the liquid over them, cover with a clean dish towel, and let steep overnight.

5. Remove the leaves and pour the liquid into sterilized bottles (see page 12). It will keep in a cool, dark place or in the fridge for up to 2 months.

## Now try this

As an alternative to serving this as a drink, use it to flavor a sponge cake. Place a few geranium leaves in the bottom of the greased cake pan, then pour the cake batter on top. When the cake has been baked and cooled, remove the leaves from the bottom, turn the cake right side up, and ice it with a mixture of confectioners' (icing) sugar and the undiluted geranium lemonade.

# Limeade

There is no harm in cheating a little every now and then, so I suggest that you save yourself a lot of time and expense by using purchased, bottled, unsweetened lime juice—available in supermarkets—for most of the juice required for this recipe. Adding the flesh of the three fresh limes required will give this lovely, refreshing drink some depth. Garnish each glass of diluted limeade with a slice of lime. For a grown-up drink, combine some of the limeade with vodka, then fill up with sparkling water as usual.

Preparation: 30 minutes

Cooking: 25 minutes

Makes about 5 cups (1.2 liters)

### INGREDIENTS

zest of 3 limes

1 3/4 cups (400g) superfine (caster) sugar

1 teaspoon citric acid

2 1/3 cups (550ml) water

2 1/3 cups (550ml) lime juice (20–25 limes, or 3 limes used for zest plus purchased lime juice to fill)

1. Put the lime zest, sugar, citric acid, and water in a pan and bring to a boil. Simmer, stirring, until all the sugar has dissolved.

2. Add the lime juice, including some of the flesh if you prefer the limeade to have a little texture, and bring back to a boil, stirring constantly.

3. Remove from the heat and allow to cool for 1 hour.

4. Pour the liquid into sterilized bottles (see page 12). It will keep in a cool, dark place or in the fridge for up to 2 months.

# Elderflower lemonade

I love to use elderflower in many different drink recipes; it gives a beautiful flowery edge—though a very subtle one in this lemonade. If you want to use these wonderful flowers in a recipe, you'll need to be quick, as their season is fleeting. Dilute with still or sparkling water or chilled white wine and soda.

**1.** Put the lemon zest, sugar, and water in a pan and bring to a boil. Simmer, stirring, until all the sugar has dissolved.

**2.** Add the lemon juice and bring the mixture back to a boil, stirring constantly.

**3.** Remove from the heat and allow to cool for 1 hour.

**4.** Put the elderflowers in a large bowl. Pour the liquid over the flowers, cover with a clean dish towel, and let steep overnight.

**5.** Strain the liquid through a fine sieve (see page 12) and pour into sterilized bottles (see page 12). It will keep in a cool, dark place or in the fridge for up to 2 months.

Preparation: 20 minutes

Cooking: 20 minutes

Makes about 5 cups (1.2 liters)

### INGREDIENTS

zest of 1 unwaxed lemon

1³/₄ cups (400g) superfine (caster) sugar

2¹/₃ cups (550ml) water

2¹/₃ cups (550ml) lemon juice (about 12 lemons)

6 heads of elderflower (see page 11)

# Orangeade

Preparation: 30 minutes

Cooking: 25 minutes

Makes about 5 cups (1.2 liters)

INGREDIENTS

zest of 2 oranges

1 3/4 cups (400g) superfine (caster) sugar

1 teaspoon citric acid

2 1/3 cups (550ml) water

2 1/3 cups (550ml) freshly squeezed orange juice (about 12 oranges)

I sometimes like to use blood oranges for this syrup, because the color is so wonderful; but don't worry if you can't find these—ordinary oranges will taste just as good. This drink is fun and simple to make and is great for brunch or an afternoon party.

I. Put the orange zest, sugar, citric acid, and water in a pan and bring to a boil. Simmer, stirring, until all the sugar has dissolved.

2. Add the orange juice, including some of the flesh if you prefer the orangeade to have a little texture, and bring the mixture back to a boil, stirring constantly.

3. Remove from the heat and allow to cool for 1 hour.

4. Pour the liquid into sterilized bottles (see page 12). It will keep in a cool, dark place or in the fridge for up to 2 months.

### Now try this

Try freezing the diluted orangeade in little cups until it is slushy, then serving it in tall glasses with two long straws and a slice of orange on the side.

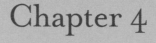

# Chapter 4

# Liqueurs

# Pear liqueur

If you've got a glut of ripe pears, this is a great way to use up some of them. For a refreshing tall drink, mix $1^1/_2$ parts of this liqueur, $^1/_2$ part Elderflower Liqueur (see opposite), 3 parts juiced cucumber (use a smoothie maker for this), and $^1/_2$ part superfine (caster) sugar, then fill up the glass with lemon soda (fizzy lemonade). Garnish with a slice each of cucumber and lemon.

I. Remove the stalks of the pears and cut them into chunks (no need to peel or core them). Put the chunks in a sterilized preserving jar (see page 12) and pour the vodka over them. Add the brandy and sugar and seal the jar.

2. Every day for a week, shake the jar to agitate the sugar. Once it has dissolved and is no longer visible, store the jar in a cool, dark place for 3 months.

3. Strain the juice through a piece of fine muslin or cheesecloth (see page 12). Discard the pulp.

4. Pour the juice into a sterilized bottle and store it for at least another 3 months. The longer you can leave it, the better the taste will be.

Preparation: 10 minutes

Cooking: not required

Makes about 3 cups (700ml)

### INGREDIENTS

9 ripe pears

3 cups (700ml) vodka

2 tablespoons brandy

$1^1/_3$ cups (300g) superfine (caster) sugar

# Elderflower liqueur

Preparation: 10 minutes

Cooking: not required

Makes about 3 cups (750ml)

### INGREDIENTS

20 heads of elderflower (see page 11)

zest of 1 unwaxed lemon

3 1/8 cups (750ml) vodka

1 1/3 cups (300g) superfine (caster) sugar

This is a fantastic liqueur with such a delicate, summery flavor you'll want to make it time and time again. It would make a perfect present for someone with a summer birthday; if it hasn't finished fermenting, just supply the instructions for finishing it and add a beautiful bottle for decanting.

I. Put the elderflower heads into a sterilized preserving jar (see page 12), and pour the vodka over them. Add the lemon zest. Seal the jar with the lid, and store in a cool, dark place for 3 months.

2. Strain the liquid through a piece of fine muslin or cheesecloth (see page 12). Pour the liquid back into the jar. Add the sugar. Return the jar to the storage place and leave it there for 2 months, shaking it once a week to help dissolve the sugar.

3. Pour the liqueur into a sterilized bottle.

# Quince liqueur

Preparation: 1 hour
Cooking: 15 minutes
Makes about 3 cups (750ml)

### INGREDIENTS

7 quinces
3$^{1}$/$_{8}$ cups (750ml) vodka
1 stick cinnamon
5 whole cloves
$^{1}$/$_{2}$ teaspoon ground nutmeg
$^{1}$/$_{2}$ teaspoon almond extract
1$^{1}$/$_{2}$ cups (350g) superfine (caster) sugar
1$^{1}$/$_{2}$ cups (350ml) water

Quinces belong to the same family (Rosaceae) as apples and pears (and roses). Although ripe quinces have a lovely aroma, they have very hard flesh and a bitter taste and so must be cooked before eating. (In Spain they are made into a paste called membrillo, often eaten with cheese.) Quinces can be hard to find. If a neighbor has a quince tree, you might beg some of the fruit; reward them with a bottle of this wonderful liqueur.

1. Grate the quinces and put them into a large sterilized preserving jar (see page 12), along with the vodka, cinnamon stick, cloves, nutmeg, and almond extract.

2. Seal the jar and store it in a cool, dark place for 3 months.

3. Strain the mixture through a double, or even triple, layer of fine muslin (see page 12); waiting for it to drip through can be time consuming, but the clear liquid is worth the wait.

4. Put the sugar and water into a pan and bring to a boil; stir until all the sugar has dissolved. Remove from the heat and allow to cool, then add it to the quince liquid.

5. Pour the liquid into sterilized bottles and cork (see page 13). It can be enjoyed immediately but will last, properly stored, as long as you like.

# Fennel liqueur

Preparation: 10 minutes
Cooking: not required
Makes about 3 cups (750ml)

INGREDIENTS

good-sized handful fennel tops (see page 11)
3¹/₈ cups (750ml) vodka
zest of 1 unwaxed lemon
1¹/₂ cups (350g) caster sugar

Once you have fennel growing in your garden, you'll have a problem knowing what to do with it—this herb grows almost like a weed. It can be used in cooking, especially with fish, but in my opinion one of the best uses is in fennel liqueur; the aniseed flavor works really well. Serve it in a small glass with a couple of ice cubes and a slice of lemon. Be warned, however: this is so good, you could end up drinking too much.

1. Roughly chop the fennel and put it into a sterilized preserving jar (see page 12), along with the vodka and lemon zest. Seal the jar.

2. Store the jar in a cool, dark place for 3 months.

3. Strain the liquid through a piece of fine muslin or cheesecloth (see page 12). Pour it back into the jar and add the sugar.

4. Store the jar for another 2 months, shaking it once a week to help dissolve the sugar.

5. Pour the liquid into sterilized bottles.

# Rose petal liqueur

Preparation: 10 minutes
Cooking: not required
Makes about 3 cups (750ml)

INGREDIENTS
......................

4¹/₂ cups (fresh) or 3 cups (dried)
(50g) rose petals

2 cups, scant (400g) superfine
(caster) sugar

3¹/₈ cups (750ml) vodka

This is a wonderful way to enjoy the beautiful summer
fragrance of garden roses while in the depths of winter. Use
highly scented pink or red roses, picking them when in full
bloom and preferably at the end of a hot day. However, you
should make sure that the roses have not been sprayed with
any chemicals; if they have, use purchased dried petals. Also,
fresh petals can produce a rather bitter taste, so you may want
to strain the liqueur earlier to prevent this if you are using
fresh ones.

1. Put the rose petals, sugar, and vodka in a sterilized preserving
jar (see page 12). Seal the jar and give it a good shake.

2. Store it in a cool, dark place for 3 months, giving it a shake
once a week to help dissolve the sugar.

3. Strain the liquid through a piece of fine muslin or
cheesecloth into a sterilized bottle (see page 12). The liqueur
is now ready for drinking.

## Now try this

You can use this liqueur to make a delicious tall drink: mix 1 part Rose
Petal Liqueur, 1 part Raspberry & Rose Liqueur (see page 91), and a tiny
drop (per serving) of vanilla extract. Fill up each glass with lemon soda
(fizzy lemonade).

# Fig leaf liqueur

This recipe came from a friend from Portugal who is a chef and who has fond memories of his aunt making the liqueur for their family. It inspired me to buy myself a couple of fig trees, which are already producing huge leaves (though small fruit). Fig trees thrive in temperate climates, but some cultivars will survive in moderately cold zones. This liqueur is a "must" for the discriminating palate and is especially good mixed with pineapple juice and ice.

1. Put the sugar and water in a pan and heat gently until all the sugar has dissolved.

2. Add the fig leaves and bring to a rolling boil. Leave it there for 15–20 minutes, then remove from the heat and allow to cool. Discard the fig leaves.

3. Add the gin and mix well. Pour the liqueur into a sterilized bottle (see page 12) and cork (see page 13). Store in a cool, dark place for at least 1 month.

Preparation: 20 minutes
Cooking: 25 minutes
Makes about 3 cups (750ml)

### INGREDIENTS

1¹/₂ cups (300g) superfine (caster) sugar

1¹/₂ cups (375ml) water

7 fig leaves (see page 11)

1¹/₂ cups (375ml) gin

# Lovage liqueur

Preparation: 20 minutes

Cooking: not required

Makes about 3 cups (750ml)

### INGREDIENTS

$^{1}/_{2}$ cup (25g) crushed fresh lovage (leaf and stem)

$^{1}/_{2}$ cup (25g) coarsely chopped fresh lovage root

1 handful fennel tops

2 cups, scant (400g) superfine (caster) sugar

$3^{1}/_{8}$ cups (750ml) vodka

Lovage has a wonderful celery-like flavor. Even if you're not overly fond of celery, do try this recipe—you may be pleasantly surprised. You could substitute brandy for the vodka; this will give a well-rounded, complex flavor, compared to the pungent, herbal flavor produced by the vodka. The liqueur can be enjoyed neat or mixed with lemon soda (fizzy lemonade).

1. Put the herbs (well rinsed) in a large, sterilized preserving jar (see page 12). Pour the sugar on top, then the vodka. Seal the jar and give it a good shake.

2. Store the jar in a cool, dark place for 3 months, giving it a shake at least once a week to help dissolve the sugar.

3. Strain the liquid through a piece of fine muslin or cheesecloth (see page 12). Pour it into a sterilized bottle and cork (see page 13). Leave it stored for as long as possible; the flavor will improve with age.

# Sloe gin

Sloes come from the blackthorn bush—a familiar sight in England, where I live, but rare in the United States. The shrub is cultivated in some northern states, however, so if you have a friend or relative who lives in those climes, you might beg some sloes from them and then thank them with a bottle of delectable sloe gin the next time you visit them. Or find a nursery in your area (if not too warm) that supplies blackthorn. Be sure, however, to wait for the first frost before picking the sloes.

1. Remove the stalks from the sloes. Then (this is the fun part) sit down, perhaps in front of the fire or the television with a mixing bowl and a sewing needle, and pierce each sloe all over.

2. Put the sloes in a large, sterilized screw-top glass jar, along with the sugar. Leave the jar in a warm place for 4 days.

3. Add the gin and store in a cool dark place for 4 months, giving the jar a shake every once in a while.

4. Strain the liquid through a piece of fine muslin (see page 12). Pour it into sterilized bottles (see page 12) and cork (see page 13). Store it for at least a year.

Preparation: 40 minutes

Cooking: not required

Makes about 5 cups (1.2 liters)

### INGREDIENTS

3 cups (750g) sloes

3¹/₂ cups (100g) superfine (caster) sugar

5 cups (1.2 liters) gin

# Sloe & cider liqueur

Preparation: 40 minutes
Cooking: not required
Makes about 3 cups (750ml)

INGREDIENTS

1¹/₂ cups (400g) sloes

1 apple

zest of 1 unwaxed lemon

1 cup, scant (100g) superfine
(caster) sugar

2 cups (500ml) gin

1 cup (250ml) (U.S. hard) cider

Sloes can be prepared by pricking them with a needle, to release their juice, but the same result can be obtained by freezing them, which simulates the first frosts, encouraging the cells inside to expand and burst. This liqueur is a great variation on Sloe Gin (see opposite) and is often enjoyed in our house over a game of cards in front of the fire.

1. Remove the stalks from the sloes and pierce them all over with a needle (or use previously frozen ones). Peel and core the apple and cut it into small chunks.

2. Put the sloes and apple into a large sterilized preserving jar (see page 12), along with the lemon zest and the sugar. Seal the jar and put it in a warm place for 4 days.

3. Add the gin and cider and store the jar in a cool, dark place for 4 months, giving it a shake once a week or so.

4. Strain the liquid through a piece of fine muslin (see page 12). Pour it into sterilized bottles and cork (see page 13). Store it for at least 12 months before trying.

# Plum & sloe gin

In this variation on Sloe Gin (see page 116), plums give a softer edge to the flavor. Use the sweeter eating plums, as cooking varieties have quite a sharp edge. If you are using produce in season, this liqueur will probably be ready in the winter of the following year, so you may wish to give it a Yuletide character by adding some spices to the blend.

1. Cut the plums in half and remove the pits. Pierce the sloes all over with a needle.

2. Put the plums and sloes in a sterilized preserving jar (see page 12), along with the lemon zest and the vodka. Seal the jar and store it in a cool, dark place for 3 months.

3. Strain the liquid through a piece of fine muslin (see page 12).

4. Pour the liquid back into the jar or into a sterilized bottle and add the sugar. Store it for another 2 months, giving it a shake once a week to dissolve the sugar. If possible, leave it for a whole year to allow the flavors to develop.

5. Pour the liquid into sterilized bottles.

Preparation: 20 minutes

Cooking: not required

Makes about 3 cups (750ml)

INGREDIENTS

10 ripe plums

1¹/₂ cups (400g) sloes

zest of 1 unwaxed lemon

3¹/₈ cups (750ml) vodka

1¹/₃ cups (300g) superfine (caster) sugar

# Spiced plum liqueur

Preparation: 10 minutes
Cooking: not required
Makes about 3 cups (750ml)

### INGREDIENTS

10 ripe plums
3¹/8 cups (750ml) vodka
zest of 1 unwaxed lemon
1 star anise
1¹/3 cups (300g) superfine (caster)
sugar

The lovely rich color and perfume of this exquisite, flavorsome liqueur help to make it a drink for special occasions, such as after Christmas dinner. Plums are available year round in supermarkets, but for best results use plums picked from your own garden or a local orchard.

1. Halve the plums and remove the pits (there is no need to peel them). Put them in a sterilized preserving jar (see page 12). Pour the vodka over it. Add the lemon zest and star anise and seal the jar.

2. Store it in a cool, dark place for 3 months.

3. Strain the liquid through a piece of fine muslin or cheesecloth (see page 12). Pour the liquid back into the jar and then add the sugar.

4. Store the jar for another 2 months, shaking it once a week to help dissolve the sugar.

5. Pour the liquid into sterilized bottles.

# Damson liqueur

Preparation: 20 minutes

Cooking: 5 minutes

Makes about 3$^1/_2$ cups (850ml)

### INGREDIENTS

2$^1/_4$ pounds (1kg) damsons

1 cup (250ml) brandy

2 cups (500ml) vodka

1$^1/_3$ cups (300g) superfine (caster) sugar

1$^1/_4$ cups (300ml) water

To make this lovely flavorsome liqueur, I include brandy, which gives a richer taste than vodka alone. You may find damsons (also called damson plums) growing wild in your area; if not, try growing some in your garden. The liqueur can be enjoyed by itself or mixed with ice and lemon soda (fizzy lemonade).

1. Halve the damsons and remove the pits. Put them, along with the brandy and vodka (well mixed) in 2 or more large sterilized preserving jars (see page 12). (You will need more than one, as you've got a lot of fruit to fit in.) Seal the jars.

2. Store the jars in a cool, dark place for 1 month.

3. Put the sugar and water in a pan and bring to a boil, stirring constantly until all the sugar has dissolved. Allow it to cool, then divide it evenly between the jars.

4. Reseal the jars and store for another 3 months.

5. Strain the liquid through 2 layers of fine muslin (see page 12), making sure you squeeze every last drop of juice from the damsons; you may need to strain again for a clearer result. Pour the liqueur into sterilized bottles and cork (see page 13). It is ready to drink but will improve if left to mature for up to a year.

# Raspberry liqueur

Preparation: 10 minutes
Cooking: not required
Makes about 1¾ cups (400ml)

### INGREDIENTS

1¾ cups (200g) raspberries

⅞ cup (200g) superfine (caster) sugar

1¾ cups (400ml) vodka

If you are lucky enough to have a plentiful supply of raspberries, save some to make this liqueur. It is a good way to preserve their flavor, and because the liqueur should be ready to drink early in the winter it will make a lovely Christmas present. I like to drink it neat, with just an ice cube, but you might like to dilute it with lemon soda (fizzy lemonade). Or try adding 1 part liqueur to 2 parts ginger beer and a squeeze of lime.

I. Put the raspberries, sugar, and vodka into a large sterilized preserving jar (see page 12). Seal the jar and give it a good shake.

2. Store it in a cool, dark place for 3 months, giving it a shake once a week.

3. Strain the liqueur through a piece of fine muslin or cheesecloth (see page 12) into a sterilized bottle. It should be ready to drink immediately.

# Raspberry & chili liqueur

Preparation: 10 minutes
Cooking: not required
Makes about 2 cups (500ml)

## INGREDIENTS

1 "Black Hungarian" chili or other small medium-hot chili

1³/₄ cups (200g) raspberries

⁷/₈ cup (200g) superfine (caster) sugar

1³/₄ cups (400ml) vodka

I love the bite in this liqueur. Because I'm not a great fan of extremely fiery chilies, I've specified a relatively mild one, but let your own taste buds be your guide.

I. Cut the chili in half lengthwise. (Wash your hands immediately after handling the chili, to avoid accidentally irritating your eyes.) Put it into a large sterilized preserving jar (see page 12), along with the raspberries, sugar, and vodka.

2. Seal the jar, give it a shake, and store it in a cool, dark place for 3 months, giving it a shake once a week.

3. Strain the mixture through a piece of fine muslin or cheesecloth (see page 12). Return the liquid to the jar or pour it into a sterilized bottle, and store it for another 3 months, if possible, to let the flavors intensify.

# Black currant liqueur

Preparation: 30 minutes
Cooking: 5 minutes
Makes about 2 cups (500ml)

### INGREDIENTS

4 cups (600g) black currants
8–10 small black currant leaves
zest of 1 unwaxed lemon
2 cups (500ml) vodka
1½ cups (350g) superfine (caster) sugar
⅓ cup (70ml) water

If you've ever drunk a Kir cocktail—or, as it's also known in France, a blanc-cassis—you will know what a rich color and flavor crème de cassis (black currant liqueur) brings to a glass of dry white wine. This recipe is my homemade take on the famous French classic. As an alternative to making a Kir, try mixing it with lime juice and lemon soda (fizzy lemonade); serve it with plenty of ice.

**1.** Remove the stalks from the currants and put them into a sterilized preserving jar (see page 12), along with the leaves and lemon zest. Seal the jar.

**2.** Store the jar in a cool, dark place for 4 months, giving it a shake once a week.

**3.** Strain the liquid through a piece of fine muslin or cheesecloth (see page 12). Discard the leaves and lemon zest. Put the currants into a blender or food processor and blitz them.

**4.** Put the liquid and the puréed currants back into the jar.

**5.** Put the sugar and water into a pan and bring to a boil, stirring constantly. Then remove it from the heat and allow to cool. Pour it into the currant and vodka mixture, stirring as you pour.

**6.** Store the jar for another 2 months, then strain the liquid again as before. Pour it into a sterilized bottle and cork (see page 13). Leave it stored for as long as possible; it will improve with age. You might like to make two batches of this liqueur: one for aging and one for drinking the first year.

# Black currant & rosemary liqueur

Preparation: 20 minutes

Cooking: 5 minutes

Makes about 2³/₄ cups (650ml)

INGREDIENTS

4 cups (600g) black currants

8–10 small black currant leaves (see page 11)

3 sprigs fresh rosemary

zest of 1 unwaxed lemon

2 cups (500ml) vodka

1¹/₂ cups (350g) superfine (caster) sugar

¹/₃ cup (70ml) water

Picking black currants is time consuming, so after all that effort you'll want to produce something fairly spectacular with them. Well, here is the perfect recipe: a gentle twist on the wonderful French crème de cassis. This is delicious with just a little ice; or you can create a stunning tall drink: place crushed ice in the glass and pour over it a shot of the liqueur. Fill up the glass with orange juice. Mix gently, so as to retain a slight definition between the colors. Enjoy.

1. Remove the stalks from the black currants and put them into a sterilized preserving jar (see page 12), along with the leaves, rosemary sprigs, and lemon zest. Pour in the vodka. Seal the jar.

2. Store the jar in a cool, dark place for 4 months. After the first month, remove the rosemary sprigs, which would otherwise give the flavor a woody tinge.

3. Strain the liquid through a piece of fine muslin or cheesecloth (see page 12). Discard the leaves and lemon zest.

4. Blitz the currants in a blender or food processor, then put them back into the jar, along with the strained liquid.

5. Put the sugar and water into a pan and bring to a boil, stirring constantly to dissolve the sugar. Allow it to cool, then pour it into the preserving jar, stirring as you pour.

6. Store the liqueur in a cool, dark place for another 2 months. Strain it again, then pour it into a sterilized bottle and cork (see page 13). Leave the liqueur to age for as long as possible.

# Lemon & thyme liqueur

If you've got some thyme in your garden, this is a good way to use this often-neglected herb. Combining it with lemons produces a lovely light drink that will not disappoint. It's wonderful just mixed with lemon soda (fizzy lemonade), but for something a little more adventurous, combine 2 parts liqueur, 2 parts gin (or whiskey), and I part Campari in a pitcher. Fill it up with lemon soda and add ice.

Preparation: 10 minutes
Cooking: not required
Makes about: 1³/₄ cups (400ml)

### INGREDIENTS

2 unwaxed lemons

5 sprigs fresh thyme

⁷/₈ cup (200g) superfine (caster) sugar

1³/₄ cups (400ml) vodka

1. Cut the lemon into slices and put them into a sterilized preserving jar (see page 12) along with the thyme, sugar, and vodka. Seal the jar and give it a good shake.

2. Store the jar in a cool, dark place for 3 months, giving it a shake once a week.

3. Strain the liqueur through a piece of fine muslin or cheesecloth (see page 12). Pour it into a sterilized bottle and cork (see page 13). Discard the lemon slices and thyme. Leave the liqueur to mature for 6 months.

# Pineapple liqueur

This is a really easy recipe, so if you come across marked-down ripened pineapples in your local supermarket, this is a perfect way to use one. Even served neat, it will conjure up images of sun-soaked days on a Caribbean island, but for a heightened fantasy experience, use it to make this long drink: mix 1 part of the liqueur, 1 part vodka, and 1 part coconut liqueur (Malibu); add a squeeze of lime and some crushed ice; fill up the glass with orange and pineapple juice; garnish with a slice of pineapple. It's your very own slice of the Caribbean.

Preparation: 20 minutes

Cooking: not required

Makes about 2½ cups (600ml)

### INGREDIENTS

1 large ripe pineapple

½ cup, scant (100g) superfine (caster) sugar

1½ cups (375ml) brandy

1. Cut off and discard the top and bottom of the pineapple and slice it thinly. Put the slices in a large sterilized preserving jar (see page 12), and sprinkle some of the sugar over it.

2. Seal the jar and leave it for 48 hours in any convenient place, such as the kitchen.

3. Press out the juice: put the slices, a few at a time, in the sieve and press down on them; or put them into a piece of muslin or cheesecloth and squeeze out the juice. Return the juice to the jar. Discard the pineapple slices.

4. Add the rest of the sugar and the brandy to the jar. Seal it and leave it in a cool, dark place for 1 month. It will then be ready to drink, though it will benefit from longer storage.

# Rhubarb & vanilla liqueur

This is a marvelous way to use rhubarb, preserving its flavor long after its growing season has ended. This recipe is perfectly balanced; but beware: it's a little too easy to drink, as it is so sweet. Try to leave it alone for at least a year to let the flavors develop. (Though we have been known to drink it all even before straining it—that's how good it is!)

Preparation: 15 minutes
Cooking: not required
Makes about 2 cups (500ml)

### INGREDIENTS

........................

1/2 pound (230g) rhubarb

1 cup (225g) superfine (caster) sugar

half a vanilla bean

2 cups (475ml) vodka

I. Chop the rhubarb finely and put it in a sterilized preserving jar (see page 12).

2. Add the sugar, put on the lid, and give the jar a shake to distribute it throughout the rhubarb.

3. Add the half vanilla bean and the vodka. Seal the jar and store it in a cool, dark place for 3 months. Shake once a week or until all of the sugar has dissolved.

4. Strain the liquid through a piece of fine muslin or cheesecloth (see page 12), pour it into a sterilized bottle, and cork (see page 13). Store for at least a year.

# Strawberry & mint liqueur

Preparation: 15 minutes

Cooking: not required

Makes about 2 cups (500ml)

## INGREDIENTS

1³/₄ cups (200g) strawberries

1³/₄ cups (400ml) vodka

⁷/₈ cup (200g) superfine (caster) sugar

4 sprigs of fresh mint

I like to grow lots of strawberries in the garden, and if I'm lucky there will still be some uneaten at the end of the summer which I can use for this liqueur—a "must-have" in our house. For a lovely summertime drink, perfect for a barbecue, combine I part liqueur with 2 parts chilled white wine and add lemon soda (fizzy lemonade) to taste.

I. Hull the strawberries and cut them into quarters. Put them into a sterilized preserving jar (see page 12). Add the vodka, sugar, and mint. Seal the jar and give it a good shake.

2. Store it in a warm place for 3 months, giving it a shake once a week.

3. Strain the liquid through a piece of fine muslin or cheesecloth (see page 12). Pour it into a sterilized bottle, and cork (see page 13). The liqueur is ready to drink immediately.

# Lavender liqueur

Preparation: 10 minutes
Cooking: not required
Makes about 3 cups (750ml)

INGREDIENTS

50 lavender heads (see page 11)
2 cups, scant (400g) superfine
(caster) sugar
3¹/₈ cups (750ml) vodka

I first tasted this amazing liqueur in Provence, France, where the fields were full of swathes of sun-drenched lavender. I make some year after year to recapture that glorious image. Although it is lovely by itself, served with an ice cube, try it also added to Champagne or other sparkling wine (I part liqueur to 3 parts wine) for a special occasion. Divine!

I. Put the lavender heads, sugar, and vodka into a large, sterilized preserving jar (see page 12). Seal the jar and give it a good shake.

2. Store it in a cool, dark place for 3 months, giving it a shake once a week.

3. Strain the liquid through a piece of fine muslin or cheesecloth (see page 12). Pour it into sterilized bottles and cork (see page 13). Although it will be ready for drinking immediately, it will improve with age.

## Lavender & peppercorn or Lavender & guava liqueur

Lavender is surprisingly versatile as an ingredient and I have several variations of the above recipe. For the braver among you try adding 15 crushed green peppercorns to the other ingredients in step 1. Leave it for at least 6 months before drinking. Trust me, the result is sublime: delicate, but with a fiery bite on the finish.

Alternatively, for a surprisingly light, refreshing drink ,cut 1 guava fruit into chunks and add it to the other ingredients. Again leave for at least 6 months to mature. It will taste fantastic with a little chilled dry white wine.

# Rose & cardamom liqueur

Preparation: 10 minutes
Cooking: not required
Makes about 3 cups (750ml)

### INGREDIENTS

10 cardamom pods
4$^1$/$_2$ cups (50g) fresh rose petals
1$^3$/$_4$ cups (400g) superfine (caster) sugar
3$^1$/$_8$ cups (750ml) vodka

This is a delicious way to make the most of highly scented roses from your garden. Choose pink or red roses and make sure they are free of any chemical sprays; pick them at their prime, at the end of a hot summer's day, when the oils will be at their most potent. The resulting liqueur is delightfully summery but not overpoweringly floral. Mix a little with some chilled white wine.

1. Crush the cardamom pods gently, using a mortar and pestle; you need only to split them, not reduce them to a powder.

2. Put them in a large sterilized preserving jar (see page 12), along with the rose petals, sugar, and vodka. Seal the jar and give it a good shake. Store it in a cool, dark place for 3 months, giving it a shake once a week.

3. Strain the mixture through a piece of fine muslin or cheesecloth (see page 12). Pour it into sterilized bottles and cork (see page 13).

4. Store the liqueur for another 3 months before trying.

# Apple liqueur

This is a good one to sip on nights in front of the fire. I love the spicy tones of the cloves and cinnamon and nutmeg and the delicious flavor of the apples. If you find that the apples you have are too tart, add a little more sugar. This liqueur is best enjoyed at room temperature by itself.

I. Core the apples, peel and slice them, and put them in a sterilized preserving jar (see page 12).

2. Add the vodka, brandy, cinnamon sticks, cloves, and nutmeg. Seal the jar and store it in a cool, dark place for 2 months.

3. Put the sugar and water in a pan and bring to a boil. Simmer until the sugar has dissolved. Remove from the heat.

4. Strain the contents of the jar through a piece of fine muslin or cheesecloth (see page 12). Put the apple pulp into the muslin and squeeze to extract all the juice. Discard the pulp and spices.

5. Pour the liquid and the sugar syrup into the jar and mix the contents well. Then pour it into a sterilized bottle, cork (see page 13), and store for at least 3 months before serving.

Preparation: 20 minutes
Cooking: 5 minutes
Makes about 2³/₄ cups (650ml)

INGREDIENTS

2³/₄ pounds (1.2kg) sweet apples

I cup (250ml) vodka

1³/₄ cups (400ml) brandy

2 sticks cinnamon

10 whole cloves

¹/₂ teaspoon ground nutmeg

I cup, rounded (250g) superfine (caster) sugar

I cup (200g) brown crystal (demerara) sugar

⁷/₈ cup (200ml) water

## Now try this

For a little extra kick, add it to a hot punch: combine 1¹/₄ cups (300ml) each of apple juice and (U.S. hard) cider, a small bag of mulling spices, and 4 teaspoons of brown/brown crystal (demerara) sugar in a pan and bring to a boil. Add a little of the liqueur to each cup.

# Mulberry & borage liqueur

Borage is a much-overlooked herb, which is a pity, as its stem, leaves, and beautiful flowers are all edible. In this liqueur, the leaves give a delicate cucumber taste, softening the tartness of the mulberries. If you can't get mulberries, raspberries (4½ cups [500g]) can be substituted. Serve the liqueur with ice cubes, sprinkled with a few borage flowers.

**I.** Put all of the ingredients into a large sterilized preserving jar (see page 12). Seal the jar and give it a good shake.

**2.** Store the jar in a cool, dark place for 2 months, giving it a shake once a week.

**3.** Strain the liquid through a piece of fine muslin or cheesecloth (see page 12). Pour it into a sterilized bottle and cork (see page 13).

**4.** The liqueur will now be ready for tasting, though leaving it to age for a few months will produce a richer flavor.

Preparation: 30 minutes
Cooking: not required
Makes about 2 cups (500ml)

INGREDIENTS

4 cups (500g) mulberries

2 cups (500ml) brandy

I cup, rounded (250g) superfine (caster) sugar

20 young borage leaves (see page II)

I star anise

# Coffee & cherry liqueur

Preparation: 20 minutes
Cooking: 15 minutes
Makes about 3 cups (750ml)

INGREDIENTS

4 cups (500g) black cherries

1 stick cinnamon

2¹/₂ cups (600ml) vodka

1 tablespoon instant coffee

1 cup, rounded (250g) superfine (caster) sugar

1 cup (250ml) water

This is a really thick, luxurious liqueur, perfect as an after-dinner drink, which is relatively easy to make and would make a welcome gift for a coffee lover. Frozen cherries can be substituted if fresh ones are out of season. Experiment with different types of coffee—instant or ground.

1. Crush the cherries by hand (wearing rubber gloves, if you like, to avoid staining your hands) in a mixing bowl, removing as many of the pits as possible (any remaining will be strained out). Put them, along with the cinnamon stick and the vodka, in a sterilized preserving jar (see page 12) and seal.

2. Store the jar in a cool, dark place for 2 months, giving it a shake once a week to prevent settling out.

3. Put the coffee, sugar, and water into a pan and bring it to a boil, stirring constantly until all the sugar has dissolved.

4. Allow to cool, then add it to the jar and store for another 2 months.

5. Strain the liqueur through 2 layers of fine muslin or cheesecloth (see page 12), pour into sterilized bottles, and cork (see page 13). It is ready to drink now but will improve if left for a couple of months to allow the flavors to mature.

# Blueberry liqueur

If you are lucky enough to grow your own blueberries or find a source of wild ones, you are in for a treat. However, you should freeze them before using them, as fresh ones tend to produce less flavor. Serve this neat as an after-dinner drink or serve it with crushed ice and lemon soda (fizzy lemonade).

I. Defrost the blueberries thoroughly and mash them with the back of a fork to release as much juice as possible. Place them in a large (1 quart [1 liter]) sterilized preserving jar (see page 12), along with the lemon zest, nutmeg, cloves, and vodka.

2. Seal the jar and store it in a cool, dark place for 3 months, giving it a shake at least once a week.

3. Put the sugar and water into a pan and bring to a boil, stirring to dissolve the sugar. Allow it to cool, then add it to the preserving jar. Mix it well with the blueberry liquid. Store the liqueur for another 3 months.

4. Strain the liqueur through 2 layers of fine muslin or cheesecloth (see page 12) and pour it into sterilized bottles, and cork (see page 13). It can be drunk now but will improve if left to mature for up to a year.

Preparation: 20 minutes
Cooking: 15 minutes
Makes about 3¹/₃ cups (800ml)

INGREDIENTS

3³/₄ cups (500g) frozen blueberries
zest of ¹/₂ unwaxed lemon
¹/₂ teaspoon ground nutmeg
4 whole cloves
3 cups (750ml) vodka
1¹/₂ cups (350g) superfine (caster) sugar
1¹/₂ cups (350ml) water

# Orange & clove liqueur

Preparation: 10 minutes

Cooking: not required

Makes about 3⅓ cups (800ml)

### INGREDIENTS

6 large oranges, zest and flesh

1⅓ cups (300g) superfine (caster) sugar

small bunch cilantro (fresh coriander), about 6 or 7 stalks with leaves

10 whole cloves

3⅛ cups (750ml) vodka

This liqueur evokes the coziness of Christmas—the feeling of overindulgence that we all succumb to every year. The cloves alone provide a spicy kick, but you might like to experiment with other Christmassy flavors, such as cinnamon and nutmeg. Serve this liqueur neat, at room temperature, or add it to black coffee for an after-dinner treat.

1. Peel the zest from the oranges and put it in a large sterilized preserving jar (see page 12).

2. Remove and discard the white pith and blitz the orange flesh in a blender or food processor. Add it to the jar, along with the sugar, cilantro (coriander), cloves, and vodka.

3. Seal the jar, give it a shake, and store it in a cool, dark place for 4 months, giving it a shake once a week until all the sugar has dissolved.

4. Strain the mixture through a piece of fine muslin or cheesecloth (see page 12) and return the liquid to the jar or to a sterilized bottle sealed with a cork (see page 13). Store it for another 8 months, if possible—though a few sips along the way to check proceedings will not do any harm!

# Blackberry whiskey

Preparation: 30 minutes
Cooking: not required
Makes about 3 cups (750ml)

INGREDIENTS

5¹/₂ pounds (2.5kg) blackberries

1¹/₈ cups (250g) superfine (caster) sugar

3¹/₈ cups (750ml) whiskey

I look forward all year to blackberry picking season, treasuring those lovely late summer/early fall days. My blackberry source is well away from traffic—an important consideration. Use good whiskey for this recipe, as a cheap one would spoil the result. I find Scotch or Irish whiskeys work better than bourbon. With a little age, this recipe produces a superb drink—well worth the wait. Drink it by itself; it's too good to mix with anything else.

I. Put the berries into a large, sterilized preserving jar (see page 12). Pour in the sugar, cover the jar, and give it a good shake to distribute the sugar throughout the berries.

2. Pour in the whiskey, seal the jar, and store it in a cool, dark place for 3 months, giving it a shake once a week.

3. Strain the liquid through a piece of fine muslin or cheesecloth (see page 12), and pour it into a sterilized bottle. Store it for at least a year before serving.

# Melon & marrow rum

I got this recipe from my grandmother. She would hang the filled marrows and melons in old stockings in the greenhouse and let the liquid drip into a bucket, covered with a piece of muslin, underneath. This makes a strong rum, so be warned! Although it's fantastic neat, you may prefer to dilute it with lemon soda (fizzy lemonade) or cola.

**I.** Slice off the tops of the marrow and melon so that they form lids. Scrape out the middles (i.e. the seeds).

**2.** Mix the two sugars and pack the mixture into the cavity of the melon and marrow. Hang these up together, cut ends uppermost, in a jelly bag or large piece of fine muslin or cheesecloth (see page 12) suspended over a sterilized bucket. Leave them for 2 weeks.

**3.** Remove the marrow and melon from their bags. Using a skewer, pierce 4 or 5 holes in the bottom of each. Return them to the bags, suspend them over the sterilized bucket again, and leave them to drip into it.

**4.** When the dripping has stopped, after about a week, discard the melon and marrow. Add the orange juice, yeast, and yeast nutrient to the liquid. You should have about 2 cups (500ml).

**5.** Pour the liquid into a sterilized 16.9 oz (500ml) plastic bottle (the kind used for mineral water) and fit a cork and air lock, as you would for a conventional demijohn (see page 14).

**6.** When the fermentation has stopped, siphon the liquid off into a sterilized bottle (see page 12) and cork (see page 13). Store it in a cool, dark place. The longer you can leave it, the better it will be.

Preparation: 20 minutes
Cooking: not required
Makes about 2 cups (500ml)

### INGREDIENTS

1 honeydew melon

1 vegetable marrow

5 cups (1 kg) brown crystal (demerara) sugar

5$^{1}/_{2}$ cups, loosely packed (1kg) dark brown sugar

1 orange, juice only

$^{1}/_{2}$ teaspoon wine yeast

$^{1}/_{2}$ teaspoon yeast nutrient

# Basic wine-making glossary

**Aperitif** An alcoholic drink, such as wine, fortified wine, or spirit, that is drunk before a meal to encourage a good appetite.

**Aroma** The smell of a young wine.

**Body** The fullness of a wine.

**Bouquet** The smell of a mature wine.

**Carbon dioxide** A colorless, odorless gas that is released in fermentation and passes through the air lock.

**Country wine** A term used for a wine produced from fruit other than grapes and sometimes from vegetables.

**Dessert wine** A strong, full bodied, sweet wine drunk at the end of a meal with a dessert.

**Dry wine** A wine in which all or nearly all of the sugar has been used up in the process of fermentation.

**Fermentation** The process by which the yeast feeds from the sugar to produce alcohol and carbon dioxide.

**Fermenting jug** An alternative name for a demijohn.

**Fortification** The addition of a spirit to wine so as to increase the wine's strength beyond that produced by natural fermentation alone.

**Hydrometer** An instrument resembling a thermometer which allows you to measure the sugar content of the liquid.

**Lees** The deposit of solids and yeast at the bottom of the demijohn.

**Must** The accumulated ingredients, including fruit, that form the basis from which wine is made.

**Stable** Describing the state in which no further fermentation can take place.

**Sticking** A state in which fermentation has stopped before enough of the sugar has been converted.

**Ullage** The space between the top of the wine and the bottom of the cork/bung.

# Index

# Acknowledgments

I would like to thank my family and close friends for their recipes, suggestions, and keen interest in sampling the finished produce.

Thanks also to Florence, Charlie, Isabel, Oscar, and Silas, who gave me their critique of the syrups, although sometimes a little too honestly!

Thank you to Pete Jorgensen for his patience throughout the project and to Nicki for her faith in me.

I would like to extend my thanks to Gavin Kingcome and Sophie Martell for their hard work in making the whole book look fantastic.

And last but not least, a big thank you to my husband, Chris, who is always there.

Please visit www.beshlie.co.uk to read my latest blog entries.